Parenting by
Developmental Design

Parenting by Developmental Design
You, Your Child, and God

Vivian L. Houk

Foreword by Scottie May

RESOURCE *Publications* • Eugene, Oregon

PARENTING BY DEVELOPMENTAL DESIGN
You, Your Child, and God

Copyright © 2010 Vivian L. Houk. All rights reserved. Except for brief quotations in critical publications or reviews, no part of this book may be reproduced in any manner without prior written permission from the publisher. Write: Permissions, Wipf and Stock Publishers, 199 W. 8th Ave., Suite 3, Eugene, OR 97401.

Resource Publications
An Imprint of Wipf and Stock Publishers
199 W. 8th Ave., Suite 3
Eugene, OR 97401

ISBN 13: 978-1-60608-796-1

All scripture quotations, unless otherwise noted, are from the New American Standard Bible or New Revised Standard Version of the Bible.

Permission was granted for the use of the photos in the book.

Also, permission was obtained for the use of the diagram in chapter 5.

To my four grandchildren, Alex, Nick, Tyler, and Katelyn, who taught me, inspired me, and captivated my heart.

Contents

Foreword by Scottie May • ix

Preface • xi

Acknowledgments • xiii

Introduction • xv

1. The Case for Childlikeness • 1
2. Historical Views of Children • 13
3. Parental Roles in Spiritual Formation • 23
4. How Spirituality Looks in Children • 37
5. The Formation of Spiritual and Religious Language • 47
6. The Role of Child Development in Spiritual Formation • 61
7. The Rhythm of Life and Spiritual Formation • 79
8. The Role of Ritual, Symbol, and Celebration in Spiritual Formation • 95
9. The Role of the Imagination in Spiritual Formation • 107
10. Tools for Calming Fears and Healing Wounds • 125

Appendix • 143

Bibliography • 145

Foreword

BEING WITH CHILDREN MAKES me happy. I love watching them. Listening to them. Talking with them. Seeing them grow. It is easy for me to say this now as a grandmother of eight. But it was not that way for much of the time in the midst of my years of parenting my own children. Because Vivian Houk has written a wonderful book that can be a friend and companion to those in the process of bringing up children, had this book been available at that time, it would have made my job as a mom much easier. *Parenting by Developmental Design* is a helpful addition to the spate of recent books focusing on children and their spiritual lives. Because my own work focuses on the role of the church in the spiritual lives of children, I find the focus on spiritual parenting valuable and complementary.

This book addresses a much neglected yet critical area of parenting: the formation of a child's spirit. Writing from a profoundly Christian perspective, Houk helps us understand the difference between the formation and the transformation of a child. She sees the earliest years of a child's life as highly significant. As I read, I had to ask myself, "What if a child first hears the blessing of God as an infant? What if those words of blessing continue throughout the child's developing years?" Oh that I would be able to respond to those questions from my own experience, but Houk helps me know how that might have unfolded.

In her warm, welcoming writing style, Houk affirms and encourages every parent with the words, "You are not alone or incapable." All along the way, she provides hope. Yet she also points out throughout the book that the condition of the spiritual life of the parents is closely connected to that of the child.

Houk begins chapter 1 by quoting Mike Mason, who simply wrote that the way to become childlike is to love a child. And that's exactly what Jesus asks adults to do—become childlike (Matthew 18:3). Loving a child most of the time is easy, but many of us need help from people like Houk when it's not so easy. She reminds us that children have fresh, spontane-

Foreword

ous, "un-rational" connections with God that adults lose over time. Her work helps us adults regain that ability.

Rebecca Nye and David Hay, scholars in the area of children's spirituality, describe this ability of children as "relational consciousness." Adults need help in being conscious of relating to the Unseen, because part of our task, as Houk writes, is to "know how to interpret life for our children." Also, Journalist George F. Will, writing in the Washington Post, said, "Biologically, adults produce children. Spiritually, children produce adults. Most of us do not grow up until we have helped children do so."

Chapter after chapter provides her insights and practical tips as well as perspectives from experts and scholars that speak into spiritual parenting. Each chapter concludes with a series of guiding questions made rich by Houk's years of ministry experience working with young children. She also communicates life lessons she learned along the way in a humble, transparent way as a mother and grandmother. She includes positive and not so positive parenting anecdotes from young parents who are still in the thick of the journey.

Friedrich Froebel, the "father of kindergarten," wrote that children must master the language of things before they master the language of words. Many parents and people who minister with children may be surprised by such a statement, but this book helps "put flesh" on it.

Of special value will be the many chapters that focus on aspects of the spiritual for children. Even the chapter titles whet one's appetite in that direction. In her chapter on the development of children, Houk integrates those social science concepts with ways a child's faith develops and is formed. In another chapter symbols and rituals are presented as tools that facilitate not spiritual experiences but spiritual meaning. Yet another chapter helps one realize the vital role imagination plays in the spiritual life of a child in order to nurture the child's ability to love God and "see" God with her or his heart. The final chapter is a goldmine for helping adults aid children in dealing with all manner of fears that rise up in their young lives.

I have known Houk for many years. Each time we are together, I learn new things about God and about children—new insights and perspectives that I had not considered. If I failed to take good notes, some of those wise gems have been lost to me. But now, through Parenting by Design, I can take the best of Houk with me. I am grateful.

Scottie May, PhD

Preface

WRITING A BOOK WAS never part of my career plan. I was a teacher and pastor. I loved working with children and their parents. But write about it? No thanks! In fact, it never occurred to me to try. I was too busy being a wife, a parent, a teacher, and a children and family ministry pastor. That took all of my available time.

So why did I decide to write this book? Over a span of thirty-eight years as an educator and pastor, I had almost continual contact with parents. I listened to their concerns and prayed diligently for guidance when they needed counsel from me. As I listened, I found that most of their questions were about how to care for and nurture their children's spiritual lives. I answered their questions as best I could with the help of the Holy Spirit. God had a plan for me to use that knowledge in another way. I just didn't know it yet.

One night I was awakened by a very strange dream. In it, I saw a podium in the middle of a small room that was covered with a green velvet cloth and had one item on it. The item was a gold pen. My hand reached down from the ceiling and grabbed the pen. At that point I woke up, and I knew the dream had some meaning for me, but I didn't know what that meaning was. I thought about that dream for years. At times I considered it nonsense. On other occasions I tried to erase the memory, ignore it, or minimize it. After all, I was working full time, raising a family, and teaching about children's spiritual formation at conferences and seminars. There was no time to write a book.

Then I retired. I was no longer working full time, raising a family, or teaching on a regular basis. I ran out of excuses. I couldn't escape any longer if I really had a heart to obey God. So, after a lot of encouragement from parents, friends, and family, I began to write what had been on my heart for a long time.

This book is the result of that long struggle. In many ways it feels like the culmination of my life's work. I still care passionately about children's spiritual formation as well as that of their parents. Because of that, I have tried to stay connected to young parents and their children in order to stay informed about God's ongoing work in them. Many of the stories in this book come directly from those obedient and loving parents who care deeply about their children's spiritual life and have been willing to share what they have learned and experienced. One mother even read every chapter as I wrote it and offered her stories and suggestions, for which I am grateful. The names of the children and parents have been changed in order to afford them anonymity.

These same parents helped me wrestle with the difficult issue of how I should make reference to a God that is both male and female. It was very difficult for me to make that determination. I believe so strongly that there are both female and male characteristics of God, but we have no word in the English language to adequately describe Him. It is sad, because all children need to know the female God as well as the male. It is a mystery we will not fully understand in this life.

Because I had to make a choice, I chose to refer to God using the masculine form in order to be consistent. It is my hope that, as parents, you will take this seriously and help your child learn to know God as both male and female: a loving Father as well as a nurturing and creative Mother. If you are interested in exploring it further, I suggest you read the book *Heart Talks with Mother God* by Bridget Mary Meehan and Regina Madonna Oliver. I believe it is biblically accurate and age appropriate. It is an excellent resource, appropriate for both boys and girls.

God bless you as you learn more and more together about this mysterious and marvelous God we all worship together.

Acknowledgments

My thanks go to many young parents who gave me permission to tell their stories in this book. I want to thank the first two critical readers, Jaime Gjerdingan and Cyd Haynes, who field-tested the material with several parenting groups and encouraged me to write the book. Also, I am grateful for Greta Richard, my daughter, who carefully read the manuscript and offered suggestions as well as editing help and encouragement. My thanks also go to Hallie Kapsner, who synthesized my vast notes so that I could include some of the material in the book. I am grateful for the children who gave me permission to share their stories. Thanks to my Community at Abbey Way Covenant, who supported and encouraged me through the whole process. Thanks go to my copyeditors, Mary Beth Curran and Julie Coleman, who helped me prepare the manuscript for publishing. And to my wonderful husband, who set up a place for me in his office space to write, unhindered and uninterrupted. Everyone's contributions have been vitally important and is much appreciated.

Introduction

Parenting is hard work. There is no getting around that. It just is! As we all know, a newborn child does not come into this world with a manual tied around his or her wrist. To support parents, many authors have written comprehensive manuals that cover the physical, emotional, and social care of children as well as development in all major areas of growth.

The area of spiritual development or formation could be, I believe, the least understood and most confusing area of parenting today. That is why I have written this book, *Parenting by Developmental Design*. I hope to offer a voice of affirmation for those who are actively engaged in finding a pathway of spiritual formation for their children. For those who have no idea how to begin, I want to offer hope and encouragement. God has given us some amazing and powerful tools, which are useful and effective in providing direction for those of us who suffer from the fear of failure or incompetence. You are not alone or incapable.

In order to facilitate your reading and understanding of this book, I need to define two terms for you: formation and transformation. I will start with formation.

A child born into this world comes with the image of God impressed upon the heart. The child has cell memory from being held and formed in the hand of God. From the moment of birth, the human child will thirst and hunger for the One they were created to relate intimately with from the beginning of time. At no other time in the child's life will they be so aware of God. The newborn or young child has no vocabulary to describe this sense of being and hence needs an adult to provide the nurture for what comes naturally in their nature. Their experiences of God need to be named. The thin places where God's work and revelation to us is visibly present need to be noticed together. The basic needs of love and protection need to be met in order to continue giving what God's loving hand provided in their formation.

This awareness of God needs to be given opportunity for expression in all kinds of ways: joy, wonder, appreciation or thankfulness, presence, and unconditional love, etc. These are all things that come so naturally for the young child and can be kept alive for a lifetime of love and adoration

Introduction

for their maker. Children need to be taught how to keep the light of Christ in them from getting smudged out by all the sin and darkness in their life and world.

Therefore, the adult community they live and celebrate the life of God with needs to help them know and see what is right and what is wrong. Until they have reached the state in their life where they know right from wrong and can reason or think abstractly, they are considered to be in their spiritually formative years. Our desire, as parents, is to see Christ fully formed and shining in their lives.

Transformation happens in a person's life when the movement of God's spirit in them causes conviction and a desire to change the course of their lives. All of us have choices to make about which path we will take from the moment we are capable of reason and abstract thinking. But making this kind of a turnabout change is something that we are not able to do for ourselves. Only with Christ's gift on our behalf can we accept God's presence in our lives, making it possible to change and walk a new path hand in hand with Him. The power of the Holy Spirit that indwells us makes transformation possible. The light and life of Christ can once again shine through us and affect the world around us and our relationships in it.

As Brennan Manning says in *Ruthless Trust*, the natural order for the formation of faith would be the development of a firm foundation of trust, faith, and then hope that guides a person in life. When this order is disrupted and one needs transformation, the order is upset. Now, faith must come as a gift from God and is followed by a new hope. Trust finally follows. It is a disrupted order but can be restored because of God's grace and mercy. Thus, a person's life is transformed.

At Abbey Way Covenant Church, where I attend, we have children in the formation stages and older ones needing transformation. None of us will be fully formed into Christ's likeness until we are in God's presence in the next life. But we do hold on to that hope as we live out our lives as God's people and support one another in the formation and transformation processes.

Because a parent's spiritual life is tied so closely to that of their children, I feel it is necessary to address the parents about their own spiritual lives first. Clearly, a parent's life with God will affect their children's spiritual formation. They must have a childlike faith of their own before they can appreciate and nurture their child's faith and growth. Because of this,

Introduction

the first three chapters deal specifically with the parent's heart and understanding. It is my hope that the remaining chapters will provide some guidance for the journey with their children in God's Kingdom on Earth. May God bless you as, together with your children, you meet God with a childlike heart.

1

The Case for Childlikeness

> *At that time the disciples came to Jesus and asked, "Who is the greatest in the kingdom of heaven?" He called a little child and had him stand among them. And he said: "I tell you the truth, unless you change and become like little children, you will never enter the kingdom of heaven. Therefore, whoever humbles himself like this child is the greatest in the kingdom of heaven."*
>
> —Matthew 18:1–3

Mike Mason, in his book *The Mystery of Children*, writes, "The way to be a good parent is by growing in childlike faith and the way to become childlike is to love a child. For we take on the likeness of what we love. If we loved children more, we wouldn't mind being one ourselves." Those words were exciting and encouraging to me because loving my children was something I understood. It required no extra reading or researching when time was so short and precious. It occurred to me that if I were to study my children I might also learn how to be a child of God. What a mystery! To paraphrase Mason, our children are bridges into that mystery. They show us how to cry out for help to the One who can help us. Children have been sent to confuse all our plans, frustrate our best interests, outwit us at every turn, drive us to our knees, and reduce us to tears. And yet, we are presented with another paradox: Children are the ones who can show us what it means to enter into the Kingdom of God as a child.[1]

---

1. Mason, *The Mystery of Children,* 81, 13.

CHILDLIKENESS

Children really know how to experience life in a way that is very different from the way we experience it. As newborns they truly reflect another world, one that they have recently known. After all, they came into this life directly from God's hand, having experienced His creative energy and life. They are fresh bearers of the image of God. In a conversation with a young mother about her child, she said that as she became more spiritually aware and connected to Jesus, her children's intimacy with God as infants and young children became evident. When she had her fourth child, they spent several days in bed together, and God's presence with the baby was palpable. The young mother was drawn to it and could hardly leave her and the Spirit's presence.

The very young have a strong capacity to accept what might seem farfetched to an adult who has much more life experience, because the veil between this world and the unseen world is so thin for children. This veil thickens over time as strands of reason, logic, and misconception get planted deeply within a person's soul and spirit. A young mother shared with me a recent experience she had with her six-year-old daughter: Her daughter kissed the air while exclaiming that God was everywhere. She believed she was kissing God. She knew He loved her always. On another occasion, this same child woke up and ran down the stairs exclaiming that she was full of God's love today. What a wonderful example of the childlike spirit in us that needs to be awakened.

I am also reminded of the story of a three-year-old girl who asked her mother if she could go into her baby brother's bedroom. Because the baby was sleeping in his crib at the time, the mother told her daughter "no." The little girl was persistent and eventually wore her mother down. Out of curiosity, the mother stood outside the baby's door, peeked through the crack, and heard her little girl say to her infant brother, "Please tell me about God. I am starting to forget."

For years I thought those kinds of spiritual experiences could only happen to well-informed and educated adults. A child would have to wait until they were intellectually capable of developing and activating that capacity out of their more adultlike understanding. My views changed dramatically after working with young children who had no trouble believing the impossible and seeing what adults couldn't see in the spiritual realm. Because of my experiences working with young children, I have come to believe that all children come directly from God's hand, full of knowledge and experience of God. They are capable of praise and worship even though they don't have understandable language to express it. Their expressions of wonder and awe at the created world are their forms of praise and worship. It is beautiful and awe-inspiring to see.

Jesus was very aware of the capacity of children for simple faith, and He often pointed adults to them as an example of the way they should approach life on this Earth. He told the disciples many times, as recorded in the Gospels, that the way into the Kingdom of God was to come as a child. I believe that children's exuberance for life, their humility, their ability (and willingness) to question anything, and their capacity to live fully in the present moment are a few of the reasons Jesus kept referring to children when speaking to the adult population. He saw their value. They were capable of pure love and devotion, something he desired from all of us.

I have summarized many of the characteristics that I believe Jesus saw and valued in children, along with ways that they express them:

Humility

- Say "I don't know" easily
- Know that some things are bigger than they are
- Know that they are little
- Can live under authority
- Become voracious learners

Dependence

- Ask for help
- Let go in order to let themselves be loved
- Are not enslaved by work; work becomes play

Questioning with a Desire to Learn

- Ask questions to understand something about the "other world"
- Challenge our picture of what life is and should be like
- Love the truth

Parenting by Developmental Design

Image-Bearing

- Take on the likeness of what they love
- Know this world is not their permanent home
- Have a proper balance of interdependence
- Trust, knowing there is grace for making mistakes
- Respond to the love of Jesus

Exuberance About Life

- Love spontaneously
- Exude excitement and enjoy life
- Enter into play completely
- Find and know joy
- Have a heart full of praise
- Exhibit radical amazement

Authenticity

- Radiate wholesome innocence; do not comprehend evil
- Exhibit naïve transparency
- Know their value to God
- Are content to be themselves
- Follow the feelings of their heart

Willingness to Forgive

- Can forgive themselves
- Extend grace
- Embrace the events of one's life uncritically

Ability to Live in the Present Moment

- Give themselves wholly
- Live in the "now"

The Case for Childlikeness

Imagination

- See God in the mundane moments of daily life
- Live in a charmed relationship with reality
- Become explorers and experimenters of the heart
- Believe in miracles and mystery
- Have adult consciousness with a child's vivid senses

An Unselfconscious Presence

- Speak God's word to adults at times
- Break the mold of the status quo
- Have sexual neutrality

Even if we, as adults, could exhibit all of these characteristics, we would still have to accept the fact that we have been born into a fallen world. This is not our true home, and the enemy is at large. But all of us come into this world with a taste for God that we never forget. It creates a longing that pulls at our hearts until we rightly connect with Him again. Children whose hearts remain open and who experience God in their early years have a much better chance of staying on the path toward God without major detours than those who lost their sense of Him in the first few years.

The following story from a wonderful young mother of four illustrates this very well:

> When my oldest child was born, my husband and I went to church but never spoke of God. I was uncertain of Him myself. By the time my daughter was six years old, we still did not have an intimate relationship with Him. He began knocking on the door of our hearts by showing us that we were losing our daughter's soul. Through several examples, He showed us that her heart was hardening. We woke up.
>
> In contrast, we did speak to our second child about God from the beginning—in all things. It was very organic, natural, and fun. By the age of two, she knew God's presence, and it was palpable to her. Once I was putting her to bed and she said with a mystical and sure air, "Mom, Jesus is here. You can go." At age nine she continues to be this way.

Parenting by Developmental Design

RESTORING THE HEART OF THE PARENT

If you have experienced love at a deep level with someone, you have found yourself thinking about that person on and off all the time. You looked forward to sharing your life experiences with that other person. You might have wondered how the other person would react to a certain situation and would have loved to watch how they handled it. Instant availability would have been great. You couldn't imagine being without your loved one in life's joyous or difficult moments.

This is what loving God with all our hearts, soul, and strength is all about. He is constantly and consistently available. He wants us to share every life experience with Him and be dependent for whatever is needed. It sounds so simple and yet seems so difficult at the same time.

If, as parents, we love God this way, He will be a part of our life with our children. It will seem as natural as drinking water is to quench our thirst. We drink in God to replenish and rejuvenate our souls so that we can continue to live the life He has called us to. Drinking Him in gives us life and energy to impart His life-giving wisdom to our children. They already know God but haven't had enough experiences to recognize Him in themselves. The parent must know how to interpret life for their children. In order to do that, an adult must live with a childlike spirit so that life with God on Earth can be modeled and explained to children in ways they can understand and accept.

Hannah, a young mom, told me this story:

> As a mom, I yearned for a childlike spirit. I wanted to be a mama with a dancing heart. But I was far from that. I was responsible, serious, dependable, and not fun. I was a good mom, but I was not like a child—I never lived in the moment, I never fully trusted, I never really lived. It took six years of inner healing with Jesus to clean out my wounds that blocked me from being like a child. But He did it! And now my children and I can experience joy while walking with God. As my trust in God grows, so does my children's faith. It happens every day.

From time to time, we need to examine our lives to see how we are doing on this path toward childlikeness. This examination does not have to take us to a place of guilt or recrimination. God's love is so big and full of understanding that He will forgive our shortcomings and give us the courage and strength to try again. If we recognize our littleness and incapacity to do right, God will work through us to do it His way. We are to direct our children to God as the source of life, rather than to ourselves. Another young mother, Carol, told me the following story:

> There is only one thing that I can confidently say makes me a good mother. When I try and try, I fail and fall short. But what helps me know that I am the best mom I can be is that at all times I point my child to Jesus. How often our world teaches us as parents that we must appear to our children as worthy of the authority God bestows on us and as somehow qualified to be in control of their little lives. We are neither worthy nor qualified. We are simply chosen and appointed and must take our post with humility, knowing that in every breath our single most important task is to point our child to Jesus . . . to His perfect love, to His safety, to His never-failing gentleness, and to His touch . . . a touch that heals from where our own impatience and imperfections have hurt our child's heart in ways we perhaps don't notice or somehow minimize in importance. That moment is an opportunity to point our children to Jesus. And Jesus is *everything* that they need in every situation. Jesus is *always* the answer to every life moment.

Real-life examples help us see that a life lived humbly and openly before God can reap great rewards. Admitting to our children that we are wrong can be difficult to do, but it gives them an example of right living for their own lives. Another young mother shared with me the following story about a difficult morning while she was home schooling her kids:

> A house divided against itself will crumble, I thought, listening again to the bickering between my three older children while the baby sat in her highchair nuzzling a bottle. I thought about the sermon I'd heard over the weekend about the division in the church of Corinth. Frustrated and at a loss, I gathered my grumbling brood and sat them at the kitchen table so I could read a portion of Corinthians to them.
>
> While I was reading, my eleven-year-old, Matthew, grinned goofily at me. I glared at him. He said, "What? I can't even smile at you, Mom?" My second son, James, who is eight, got up from the table to hug me, and I reluctantly hugged him back. He went away in a huff. He sat on the couch and said, "You're mean, Mom. I don't want to listen to you."
>
> Once I got him back seated with his siblings again, I angrily bound the spirit of division in Jesus' name. My son, Matthew, rolled his eyes and said, "You are the worst of us, Mom!" I swallowed the

jab and started reading from the Bible again. Two verses later, James bopped his five-year-old sister, Rachael, in the head. In utter frustration, I tossed water at him. He ran around the room wailing in outrage. Pushed to the limit, I shouted up to God. "Could you give me a little help here? I do want to do this for you!" I sat down in my chair hopeless and helpless. I said, "We should all just pray quietly."

Matthew said, "I pray we have a good day." James said, "I don't want to pray." He crossed his arms over his chest and frowned at me. I sat silently, thinking, "I'm hopeless. This is hopeless. I do want them to understand that we are being divisive. What am I supposed to do?"

While I was brooding, Matthew started singing a praise song. Halfway through the song, I joined him. I led us through two more songs, with James and Rachael adding their voices. And in the middle of the final song, about finding a heart for worship, Matthew got up to clean the kitchen. Rachael started dancing and then went to play the piano. James hugged me tightly, and while I squeezed him close, I prayed, "Lord, this isn't how I had wanted it to go." I heard His chuckling answer in my heart: "But it is the way I wanted it."

I thought about how I had handled the morning, and a flush of embarrassment spread over my face. "I'm sorry I got so angry with you, James." He grinned at me and said, "That's okay, Mom." I looked at my baby daughter, Elisabeth, in her highchair and admired her golden curls and blue eyes. What did she think of all the commotion? I sighed. Would I ever figure out this motherhood thing? I listened to Rachael singing, "Butterflies are rainbowy. That's what makes them so pretty. I love God, and God loves me." I smiled, squeezing James tight before releasing him to play.

"I'm sure sorry I messed it up, Lord." As the confession spilled from my heart, the Holy Spirit revealed truth. My children are beautifully unique. They responded to the Lord's call to worship Him in the ways they most naturally do. How often in a day do I find Matthew cleaning the kitchen even when I haven't told him to do it? How often do I find Rachael at the piano playing and singing or at the table coloring a picture? How often does James hug me? I have a server, an artist, and an exhorter in my home. Who knows what the baby will grow into?

To find the heart of worship in my home, I must embrace the differences in my children and fan their passion for God in ways they understand. To force them to worship the Lord my way—with a Bible, a pen, and words—squelches the Spirit's movement.

The Case for Childlikeness

> When I finally gave up control this morning, God stepped in. He pointed out to me that He loves my children's spiritual life more than I do. It was a humbling thought. He said then that He cares for unity in my home more than I do, and sometimes the solution is getting the mom out of the way and putting me back into place as His child first.
>
> I smiled, realizing how foolishly I had behaved that morning. I had been, as my oldest son so sagely said, "the worst of all of us." I had to admit to myself then and there that sometimes I am the biggest culprit for division in my home. I never want to be the root of the problem, but the sin in me stirs up all that I don't want to be. Only beautiful sweet grace, which flows from God to me and then through me to my family, unites a home and gives it a heart for worship.

I wonder what her children will remember about that day. What will they know about God? Only time will tell. Regardless of whether they can recall any details about that incident or not, it was formative. I love what author, Macrina Wiederkehr, says about her childhood experiences:

> The spirituality of my childhood is the one I would most like to have restored. It was pure and fresh and honest. I read God everywhere! It was Divine Reading at its best. The forest was my place of solitude. The trees, like gods and goddesses, bent down to hear my prayers. I trusted them with all the secrets of my heart, and I was never disappointed. In their presence I felt safe. Looking back at the poverty and the wealth of my childhood, my memory becomes a ray of hope and pain. I have become too complicated in my prayer. Yet under the eye of God all shall be restored.[2]

As Wiederkehr says in her poem, *Is There a Lost Child in You?*, what disturbs her most is the inability to reach back into her childhood and recapture what she was as a child.

Developing new skills always takes practice and time. In fact, it takes twenty-one days for a practice to become a habit. Short of a miracle, changes in our parenting won't happen overnight. We have to consistently practice a new skill.

In the spiritual realm, real inward change won't happen unless God does it. So, in addition to mindful practice, hearts need to be rejuvenated by the Holy Spirit. He does that in His own way when we come with will-

---

2. Wiederkehr, *A Tree Full of Angels*, 62–63.

ing hearts and lay down our own need for control. Then God is free to work His transforming power in us.

Exercise and practice help us change and grow. So, if you are interested in giving it a try, choose an exercise from the following list; one that appeals to you. Ask God to join you as you practice the one(s) you have chosen.

1. Make a list of childlike behaviors you wish you still had. Make a point of looking for them in your children while praying that God would grow them in you again. Mark occurrences on a calendar or in a journal so you can see God's handiwork in you. Communicate to your children your appreciation for what you see in them.

2. Try stopping what you are doing in any given moment to ask God what He is doing now. Note His responses in your heart and mind and then continue what you were doing. Do this throughout your day. When you are comfortable with the process, teach your children to do the same thing. Make it a rhythmic practice, and don't feel like you need to talk about it out loud each time.

3. Try to discover for yourself when and where you most easily feel in touch with God. Open yourself to stretch for the same kind of connection in other areas of your life.

4. Invite a trusted friend to join in a particular experience with you. Note how your experiences are the same or different. Remember, God loves variety and planned the world accordingly.

5. Pay attention to the environment you create for your children. Is there ample room for questioning? If not, partner with God to change it, and watch what happens.

6. Make a mark on a paper for the number of times you think of God during the day. Periodically check yourself and see if there is a change from when you began.

7. Note the lies that come into your mind, and turn to Jesus when they come. What do you notice when you regularly do this?

Most of all, I want parents to know that ultimately God is in charge, and they should depend upon Him just as their children depend on them.

The Case for Childlikeness

Dependence does not come easily to adults. For children, it is a way of survival. Maybe that is the way to look at it. Children use the word "help" easily. I believe God loves to hear us speak that word. Use it frequently and openly. You will not be sorry, and both you and your children will benefit from your willingness to be vulnerable in this way.

In summary, we are called to love the childlike spirit in our children and to desire it for ourselves. When I read the accounts of Jesus in the Book of Matthew, I can see very clearly that Christ understood the dispositions and nature of children. When Jesus called children, they gave Him their trust; when children were brought to Jesus, they gave Him their love; and when children were aware of Jesus' presence, they gave Him their worship. Jesus wisely decided to reveal himself in a manner that invited children to respond, free from undue pressure or persuasion. As adults, we can respond to God openly and freely in the same manner. Our children can lead the way.

2

Historical Views of Children

Then God said, "Let us make man (human beings) in Our image, according to Our likeness."

—Genesis 1:26a

THE WAY THAT WE see children affects how we will parent them. If we see them as "less than," we will treat them accordingly. If they are valued as spiritual beings with capabilities worth desiring for ourselves, we will treat them with respect and learn from them.

The value and capabilities of children has been a controversial subject for many years. Views have varied according to the historic time period and the culture. J. Philip Newell, a twenty-first-century Scottish theologian, writes, "Well into the 19th century, there was a belief that in the birth of a child the image of God is being freshly born among us. This was to speak not simply of what is true of a child but of what is most deeply true for all people and for all creation. God is the Life within all life."[1] Thus, all that has life is sacred.

There was a time when children were needed as laborers in order for a family to survive. While that may still be true for some families today, American child labor laws prohibit the abuse of children in the workplace. Children are capable of learning valuable skills and working very hard, but they must play in order to achieve healthy development.

In contemporary Western culture we value the childhood stage of life, but we seldom regard the contributions of children to our society as having much value or importance. We assign chores for the children in a family or classroom, but the completion of those jobs isn't necessary for the survival of the family or the school.

1. Newell, *One Foot in Eden*, 2.

What adults think children are capable of understanding or experiencing in the spiritual realm varies greatly from culture to culture. Cultures vary in what they teach children and expect from them in return. Some parents and teachers have children memorize a lot of religious information since memorization comes so easily for them. The idea is that children will recall what they've memorized at the time when it is needed in their life. At the opposite end of the spectrum are those who believe children are not capable of a spiritual life until they have reached the age of reason, usually at the preadolescent stage. They are not viewed as image-bearers. Therefore, there is no need to nurture their spiritual lives until they are old enough to cognitively understand and respond.

BIBLICAL VIEWS

The Bible gives us some solid historical information about how ancient Israel was supposed to value and train their children. In the Old Testament in Deuteronomy 6:6–9, God tells the Israelites to first love God with their entire being and then teach their children to do the same. They were to teach them in the everyday moments of life in their homes and throughout the community. It was the responsibility of the whole community to support the family in this way of raising children as spiritual beings. Children were included in all the ceremonies, festivals, and rituals that were a part of the Israelites' lives together in community. That included their worship, which was lived out in all their life experiences. All of their festivals and celebrations pointed toward God and acknowledged Him as the creator of the universe and the giver of all good things. They were instructed to show their children the stone markers that had been erected as reminders of God's goodness and faithfulness to them.

In the New Testament, Jesus consistently reminded His followers that children were to be valued highly. He told them that they (adults) were to come to the Kingdom of God as children if they wanted to participate in the life of the Kingdom. When the disciples tried to keep parents from taking their children to Jesus for a blessing, He rebuked them and told them to bring the children to Him. No one was too little or insignificant for Jesus to place value on them by giving them His full attention and blessing.

CLASHES OVER THE STATE OF A CHILD'S SOUL AT BIRTH

By 624 AD, differing opinions about the spiritual state of a newborn and the value of a child came to a head at the Council of Whitby in England. The Roman Church believed strongly in the doctrine of original sin, which decreed that every child was born sinful. That belief was widespread and deeply ingrained in the hearts and minds of the leaders of that church. The famous theologian, Augustine of Canterbury, "believed that from conception and birth we lack the image of God until it is restored in the sacrament of baptism, and that conception involves us in the sinfulness of nature, sexual intercourse being associated with lustful desire."[2]

In the Roman belief system there was no hope of salvation or eternal life for a young child who had not been baptized into the church. Each newborn carried the weight of the sin of generations past and needed salvation from the outside rather than from something or someone residing within them. Because children were too young to choose a life with God for themselves, it was up to the parents and the church to make that happen for them. Since infant mortality was so high in the seventh century, it was a big issue for parents of that day.

Infant baptism provided a way for parents to overcome their fear of their child's eternal damnation if they didn't survive until the age of reason. There was no hope for salvation until the child reached that age and could be taught what he or she needed to know.

The clergy held very important positions in the religious life of the laypeople, who were largely illiterate. They depended upon the clergy to be the imparters and interpreters of truth. The laity had no other way to hear the Word of God than through the mouths of priests.

People's lives at this time were divided into secular or sacred. The two did not meet in everyday life. What a contrast this was to the Israelites' belief that all of life was sacred. There was no separation. Hence, they received a direct word from God, which is recorded in Deuteronomy 6, as mentioned earlier. The Israelites were instructed to love God with all their being and to share Him with their children in the everyday course of living.

In the Roman environment, children were considered to be empty pitchers waiting to be filled or empty slates needing to be written upon. There was very little of value residing in them in their early years. They

---

2. Newell, *Listening for the Heartbeat of God,* 14.

were lovely and precious possessions but were supposed to be seen and not heard. This mindset continued for many years throughout Europe and even into the New World.

AN OPPOSING VIEWPOINT

On the other hand, Pelagius, a spokesperson from the Celtic branch of Christianity in the West during the fifth century, believed "that to look into the face of a newborn is to look at the image of God; he maintained that creation is essentially good and that the sexual dimension of procreation is God-given. The emphasis that would increasingly be developed in the Celtic tradition was that in the birth of a child God is giving birth to his image on earth."[3]

Celtic Christianity had been thriving for a long time in Scotland, Ireland, and parts of Northern Europe. Matthew Fox, who wrote *Original Blessing*, said that "These countries had been strongly influenced by the creation-centered traditions that date back to the ninth century B.C. with the very first author of the Bible, the Yahwist or J source, and including the psalms, the wisdom books of the Bible, the prophets, Jesus and much of the New Testament, and to the very first Christian theologian in the West, St. Iranaeus (c. 130–200 A.D.). The fall/redemption spiritual tradition espoused by the Roman church is not nearly as ancient as is the creation-centered one."[4]

Romans moved very strongly into the Celtic world, and they met with the leaders head-on in the Council of Whitby, as previously mentioned. There were many irreconcilable differences. One of them had to do with the Celtic view of the spiritual state of unborn and newborn children.

The Celtic Christians believed that infants were the most perfect image-bearers of God we could ever hope to see in this life. Infants had recently been in God's presence and had been formed by God's hands. Young children carried within them the light of God and reflected His character to everyone around them.

Children were regarded as the most innocent and beautiful form of human life because it was possible to experience the presence of God within them. Newell said that "birth then, whether that be our birth or

---

3. Newell, *Listening for the Heartbeat of God*, 15.
4. Fox, *Original Blessing*, 11.

the birth of any living creature, is at heart a fresh inception of God's life among us."[5]

Newell writes that Pelagius, a theologian considered by the Romans to be a heretic of great proportions, said that

> His emphasis on the essential goodness of humanity did not involve a denial of the presence of evil and of its power over the human. Rather, it implied that at the heart of humanity is the image and goodness of God, a goodness that is obscured or covered over by the practice of wrongdoing and evil. Deeper than any wrong in us is the light of God, the light that no darkness has been able to overcome, as St. John had written. At the heart of humanity is the "light that enlightens every person coming into the world." For Pelagius, evil was rather like an occupying army. The people yearn for liberation, but are bound by the forces of evil. Redemption, therefore, can be understood in terms of a setting free, a releasing of what we essentially are. Our goodness is sometimes so deeply buried as to be lost or erased, but it is there, having been planted by God, and awaits its release. For Pelagius, the redemption that Christ brings is such liberation, a freeing of the good that is in us, indeed at the very heart of life. . . .
>
> Pelagius believed in the essential innocence of a baby and the conviction that original sin is not present in the individual soul at conception. Adam's original sin, he believed, was to be seen strictly as an example of what happens when we do wrong, as opposed to being a debilitating fault that we inherit at conception."[6]

Another difference that was important in the Celts' clash with the Roman Church was their view of the natural world. Celtic Christians believed the entire natural world reflected God's glory and spoke to the people as did God's written word. God was visible in all creation and was worshipped as the Creator, giver of light and life, and redeemer. He was visible in the mundane things of life as well as in the glorious ones. There was no distinction between the secular and the sacred. This more closely reflected the viewpoint that the Israelites had when they were instructed by God during their wandering years in the wilderness.

In both the world of the ancient Israelites and that of the Celts, anyone could approach God. That privilege did not just belong to the clergy. Children, women, the rich or the poor—all had access to Him at all times

---

5. Newell, *One Foot in Eden*, 3.
6. Newell, *Listening for the Heartbeat of God*, 14–15.

of the day or night. Children heard the prayers of the people around them throughout the day, and they were included in the celebrations of the seasons and rhythms of life. Celts gave children an *anam cara,* or soul friend, when they were born. This appointed person was to act as a guide, an encourager, and a spiritual director throughout the life of the child.

Sin was still an issue to be dealt with. A child was the most innocent bearer of Christ's life and light in the world. But, because a child was born with the capacity for missing the mark, the light and life of Christ in a child would cloud over with sin, thereby dulling the reflection of the image of God. This smudging would never totally put out the light but would dull its reflection. The grace and mercy of God delivered through the life of Jesus Christ was able to cleanse and purify and to allow once again the light to shine in the dark world.

Spiritual awareness and capability will dim as a child grows if their spiritual encounters and experiences aren't named for them. While the parents' role in naming their God encounters and experiences is vital, children must be able to recognize God and fall in love with Him on their own.

OUR CHRISTIAN CULTURE'S RESPONSE TO CHILDREN

In some arenas of our contemporary Christian culture, children are considered empty slates needing to be filled. Salvation prayers recited by the very young in these churches and evangelistic groups are encouraged in order to ensure safe passage to heaven.

In other groups and faith traditions, the unique gift of childhood, their inherent spirituality, is encouraged and nourished as their experiences of God are recognized and named. They are told Biblical stories and given examples of a living God who's at work in their world today so that they might truly continue loving the God who made them and continues to care for them in very protective ways.

In other spectrums of our Christian society, the church is solely responsible for educating children about God. Parents often express that they feel unqualified to teach children about the spiritual life with God and don't know where to begin. Much of this hesitation comes from the belief that one must know correct doctrine in order to teach children or nurture the faith they already have. If the responsibility for nurturing faith is left to the church alone, much of what children receive will be "head knowledge." There will be a huge void in a child's relationship with God if that is all they get. What the child had known earlier about God is soon forgotten. Later on, in adolescence, they need to be given the opportunity to solidify and renew for themselves what they have believed to be true.

QUESTIONS TO CONSIDER

1. What did your parents believe about children's value and capabilities?
2. How did it affect you?
3. What do you believe in this regard?
4. How does this affect your parenting?
5. What do you want to do differently?
6. Whose teaching do you want to emulate?
7. Who are your role models and why?
8. What are the mixed messages you have received from your families of origin, your culture, and the church community you belong to?
9. How do we break old patterns of behavior that have been well established in our homes?
10. What does it look like to parent in a new way?

EXERCISES FOR PRACTICE

Remember that change takes time and practice. Reclaiming childlikeness as an adult is a lifelong pursuit. It involves transformation of our own hearts first. God needs to be in charge and He knows where to start.

1. Look at your children with new eyes and let them lead you to new places with God.
2. Select practices that will lead you in these new directions, whatever they are.
3. Study the scriptures that can guide you in your change process.

The Word of God to the People of God

- Deuteronomy 6:1–9
- Deuteronomy 11:19
- Deuteronomy 31:12
- Joshua 8:35
- Psalm 8:1
- Psalm 34:11
- Psalm 78:1–8
- Proverbs 22:6
- Isaiah 28:9
- Joel 1:3

Jesus' Words of Value Placed on Children

1. Matthew 18:4
2. Matthew 19:14
3. Mark 9:37
4. Mark 10:16
5. Luke 9:48

In conclusion, remember as parents that God's gift of grace brings out and releases the original goodness that is inherent in each individual but is dimmed by evil. Grace allows and enables our own natures to flourish as we cooperate with the light of the Spirit of God within us. As Newell says, "Christ is the liberator, the One who shows us the treasure that is within our lives and guides us in the way of its redemption. It is a goodness that is to be found again and again in life, in different ways and in the various dimensions of who we are."[7]

I challenge you to see what difference this view of God's grace can make in your life as well as in that of your children. In the song "Close Your Eyes So You can See" by Michael Card, we are invited to view the world through the eyes of the heart in order to see it the way it was meant to be seen. We can join our children in this way of seeing because it is so

---

7. Newell, *One Foot in Eden*, 2.

Historical Views of Children

much easier for them. When we do this, we encounter a paradox in God's plan: The path to maturity is one that encourages us to let the light of our childhood and our children shine and guide us. John, the New Testament evangelist, says in John 1:4, "In Him was Life, and the Life was the light of men (humankind)." Throughout history, despite all the changes, this truth remains and provides us, as parents, hope for all.

3

Parental Roles in Spiritual Formation

And you must love the Lord your God with all your heart, all your soul, and all your strength. And you must commit yourselves wholeheartedly to these commands that I am giving you today. Repeat them again and again to your children. Talk about them when you are at home and when you are on the road, when you are going to bed and when you are getting up. Tie them to your hands and wear them on your forehead as reminders. Write them on the doorposts of your house and on your gates.

—Deuteronomy 6:5–9

Everyone who comes into contact with a child has the potential to nurture that child's spiritual formation. Parents have the most natural connection and the best opportunities, but in this day and age, parents often relinquish this responsibility to others who have been specifically trained to nurture children's spiritual growth. The church they attend steps in to fill the gap. While the church might be the only source for spiritual guidance for some children who do not have Christian parents, I do not believe this is the plan God had in mind. He instructed us to teach our children and nurture them in the everyday events that occur in family and community life.

How does a parent go about doing this? If you believe that the God who designed us knows what is best for the children He gave us, it naturally follows that He would give us what we need to do the job. Even though a child does not come into this world with an instruction manual tied around its wrist, we are not left without available help at any hour of the day or night.

I believe the passage cited at the beginning of this chapter provides a good starting place. It paints a picture of what the ideal relationship with God looks like before giving instructions for raising a God-loving child. If your relationship with God is in order, you will more likely be able to nurture a similar relationship with God in your children because you have experienced it yourself. You can know God intimately or learn to know Him alongside your children. If you are new at this, you can grow in this relationship together with your children. Time is not an issue with God.

SACRED CONNECTORS

As you know, the job of parenting is all consuming and very difficult. So adding the responsibility of spiritual development to the demanding tasks of physical and emotional care can be daunting unless one understands the roles God calls us to as well as how they fit into everyday life. The Deuteronomy passage mentioned earlier illustrates the best way to guide your children's spiritual formation. Keeping that in mind, we will examine what I consider to be the most important roles for parents and how they might fit into life with your children today.

Young children must have every part of this life explained and named for them. You are constantly called upon to name everything they encounter in their environment. This kind of living is important because it demonstrates for a child the way to live with God as the center of their entire world. Parents are the ones best equipped to name a child's experiences and encounters with the Holy One who is called God.

I am reminded of the ancient biblical story of the very young boy, Samuel, who had been brought to the temple to be raised by Eli, the priest. As the story goes, Samuel is awakened during the night by a voice calling his name. Samuel doesn't know where that voice is coming from and it probably scares him. So he runs to Eli and tells him what has happened. Eli comforts him and sends him back to bed. After a few more times, Eli finally realizes that Samuel is hearing the voice of God but Samuel doesn't recognize it yet. So he names the experience for Samuel and tells him how to respond when he hears it again. The name he gave the voice was God. Samuel then knew how to recognize God's voice and became one of the greatest and most important prophets in that Old Testament time period.

Parental Roles in Spiritual Formation

Sleeping and dreaming are a normal part of everyday life. God chose to make Himself known to Samuel by speaking to him in the quiet of the night, but Samuel needed a parental figure to tell him who it was, what it meant, and how he should respond. One can just imagine Eli telling Samuel to go back to bed repeatedly without giving it much thought. It was Samuel's persistence that gave Eli a reason to reconsider and listen for God's prompting. He then directed young Samuel to listen for and answer God's call to him, and it changed the course of history.

Samuel did not scoff at Eli or call him old and stupid or ridiculous. He just obeyed him. He was very young, possibly four years old at the time. He did not question the directions; he just did what Eli told him to do. Children have a strong capacity to accept what might seem crazy to an adult who has much more life experience. The veil between this world and the unseen world is thin for children and much thicker for adults. It gets thick over time when strands of reason and logic get planted deeply within a person's soul and spirit.

One might be tempted to think that Samuel was just an unusual child. After all, he lived in the temple with Eli, who was a priest. How natural then for this to happen in a location that was deemed a Holy place rather than in a common or ordinary home where parents are simply parents and children are children. While we know that Samuel was called and gifted to be a prophet, I believe children in normal and ordinary homes are also sensitive to God's voice and can learn to recognize it just as Samuel did. But what they need is an adult who can name it for them so they can recognize it and respond to it on their own.

Living out the role of sacred connector can be as simple as naming God as creator, even at the youngest stages of a child's life. Most recently, I remember changing my grandson's clothing while giving God the credit for his toes and fingers, bellybutton, and chin. Another time, I had a great conversation with my three-year-old grandson about what God has made versus what human beings have made. We had been watching a butterfly open its wings and take flight for the first time. Once again, I was a sacred connector.

These are only two examples of what it might look like to be a sacred connector for your children. Every day is filled with opportunities to experience wonder and awe together as you explore the beauty of the world around you. God can easily be introduced to children as the One who made it all. Their own body parts are evidence of God's handiwork and need to be named in conjunction with God. They readily accept that truth and have no trouble believing what you say. It is something, I believe, they already know at the cell level of their being.

As a parent, you have many opportunities each day to make sacred connections for your children. Doing this might mean you have to learn a new, more mindful way of thinking about and observing life. The role of sacred connector is important and not as difficult as it may seem. It is about pointing to the evidence of God that is apparent in your everyday life and routines. Most of these experiences can be spontaneous. They are not the kinds of activities you need to plan. Just be aware of opportunities to connect with God, each other, and the world that God has created. There are no formulas for taking advantage of teachable moments. Neither are there lists of prescribed activities to do on a regular basis. You simply live life together, noticing God's handprints, while naming Him as the creator of all things.

Because God is revealed in everything that has been created and is available anytime and anywhere, children have the opportunity to experience God in a way that will stay with them for life. Children who experienced God in their early years and whose hearts have been kept spiritually open have a much better chance of staying on the path toward God without major detours than those who lost their sense of God in those first few years. They learn to recognize God by sight, sound, touch, taste, and even smell. As one five-year-old child so aptly put it, the voice of God can be heard as a "whisper across my heart and then out my head."

This way of knowing God can be likened to the way that you come to recognize your own children's presence in the home. One day when I came home from work, I entered our laundry room and noticed the signs that indicated my six-year-old daughter was home. Some of her belongings were left on the dryer. I walked into the family room and saw her sweater hanging on the back of the couch. I continued to follow the trail she had left until I found her. The clues she left allowed me to go straight to her without a detour. I knew her so well that it made it easy for me to find her. None of my friends could have done that because they hadn't lived with her and didn't know her patterns of behavior or signs of her physical presence like I did.

I remember thinking at the time how similar that kind of knowing was to the way we get to know God. When you follow His leading you come to know God so intimately that you can recognize His tracks in your life and find Him there. God is close and can be seen through the eyes of your heart. Because you know Him, you can help your children learn to recognize or read His signs as well.

If this sounds too difficult and you feel too inexperienced to do it, let me remind you that you are not alone in this role. The Holy Spirit is ready and available to help you the moment you declare your need. That is all it takes: a cry for help or a declaration of your need. Then you can confidently help your children make a sacred connection between what they have experienced and the God who is responsible for all of creation. They can know that God is always there, waiting to be loved and enjoyed. A deep faith develops that enables them to trust in the midst of good as well as bad times.

NURTURERS

Another critically important role for parents to play is that of nurturer. To nurture means to encourage growth by providing optimum conditions for healthy growth and development. It presumes that there is something already present to stimulate toward growth, rather than an empty pitcher waiting to be filled (John Locke's *tabula rasa*). Nurturing provides a framework for this style of interaction with your children in the care and development of their spiritual growth.

Nurturing provides an opportunity for children and adults to grow together, side-by-side, in an ever-changing, mutually enhancing way. One of the mothers I worked with as a pastor said it this way:

> Sometimes we make mistakes and discipline for the wrong reason or expect the wrong things from our children. Because of this, it is of vital importance that our children know (because we tell them) that we are not perfect, that we apologize when we make a mistake, and that we identify and recognize our error or mistake verbally to them. All these things are important because we model and teach our children how to identify their own wrong behavior and mistakes.
>
> But also, it is very important because it helps establish two things. First, it establishes that we are not God. Children look to us for the image of God. So, we need to teach them how to recognize when we fail to reflect God's image so that they don't cast our human image onto their belief about God and limit their relationship with God based on an untrue belief about His character. Second, it shows that we, too, are children of God who are learning to

obey Him. So, children are to obey their parents because that is the way God designed it and it is best for them. It is not because we are always right or perfect. If they understand that God calls them and instructs them to obey their parents, they will, hopefully, come to understand that by obeying their parents, they are actually obeying God. I hope that, as they become adults, they will already understand that the meaning of life is found in obeying God and loving Him the rest of their lives. Even though bad things happen in life, remaining in Jesus' love is the way we ensure that our hearts are protected from anything the evil one can do to us or throw our way.

You will find that young children hold rather primitive religious or spiritual beliefs. They are maturing in all areas of their development at a very rapid pace and often are out of sync with themselves. They may not be able to grasp many cognitive truths in their youngest years but will grow in their ability to understand as they are guided and instructed along the way. This process reminds me of the way children learn to read. They will confuse similar letters or words until they learn to recognize them consistently. When they are practicing new physical skills they will often fall down. But they get back up and try again until that skill is mastered. As a parent you get to provide the encouragement and motivation to keep your child working on the skills that will make the experience of spiritual development challenging and rewarding. That is a form of nurturing.

We have established that it is ideal for spiritual nurturing to take place in the home environment. But in addition to the time spent in their homes, children of the ancient Hebrews were invited to participate in the entire life of the community. When the community celebrated or remembered God's faithfulness, the children were an integral part of it. I love to imagine what it must have been like for the children of the Israelites to cross the Red Sea and memorialize it with stones taken from the river for an altar. What a ceremony that must have been! The community was not the principal nurturer in this example, but it certainly added experience and knowledge of God to children as they participated with others who held the same values and beliefs.

I have written about the importance of nurturance in the home and community, but what does nurturing really look like? An interesting analogy comes from the natural world. A gardener plants a seed in a place that is believed to be optimal, knowing that conditions must be right for it to grow. To facilitate that growth process, the gardener waters the ground, prays that the sun will shine, and removes weeds that would choke out the young plant, watching and waiting for it to poke out of the ground. Sometimes it is necessary to work the dirt around the new little plant so that its roots can spread and supply the plant with the nutrients it needs to grow. But a real gardener never digs up the seed or young plant prematurely to examine its progress. To uproot it at an inappropriate time would mean the new life in that plant would cease to grow.

In a similar way, your child enters life within your family. You provide the environment and optimal conditions for your child to grow into what they were created to be. Your child is protected and provided with the food, water, shelter, and care necessary for healthy growth and development.

Nurturing the spiritual life of children is as important as nurturing their physical and emotional lives since children are, first and foremost, spiritual beings. As a parent, you have a responsibility to provide an environment that promotes your child's spiritual growth: They need feeding, watering, and exposure to the Light, as well as the weed pulling, which provides correction and instruction. When the roots of a child's spiritual life grow deep and feed on the true source of creation, spiritual formation happens. It is possible to see a deep love for God and others blossom. This is the goal for parents who want to nurture a child's spiritual growth in a healthy way.

BESTOWERS OF BLESSINGS

Another way that you can participate in the spiritual formation of your child is to bestow blessings upon them. John Trent and Gary Smalley have written a book entitled *The Blessing*, which examines the Old Testament practices of bestowing biblical blessings upon children in their homes and community. These blessings could be spoken to the child alone, in the family setting, or in a community gathering.

There are five major elements or parts that make up a family blessing. The first part consists of meaningful touch. It is an essential element in bestowing a blessing. Meaningful touch provides a caring foundation to the words that will be spoken. Kissing, hugging, or laying on of hands are all ways to bestow a blessing, and have many beneficial effects. The act of touch is the key to communicating warmth, personal acceptance, affirmation, and even physical health. Therefore, touch is an integral part of any blessing.

The second part of the family blessing is a spoken message. Words of love and acceptance need to be said out loud. A blessing becomes so only when it is spoken aloud to the child. Spoken words give the hearer an indication that he or she is worthy of attention and love. In preparation for offering a spoken message, you must commit to becoming a student of your children in order to genuinely bless them. Only if we study them can we offer each of them a unique blessing that is both personal and honoring. Encourage them to walk their own honest journey while offering them the freedom to be who they really are.

As grandparents of two teenage boys, we get to bless our grandsons with words of love and affirmation on their birthdays. These letters are filled with examples of the good things we have witnessed during the year. As they continue to grow and develop they know someone is noticing them and loving every minute of it. We have written these blessings out for them so that they can be read whenever they need to be encouraged or remember that they are loved. They have special boxes designated for storing these words of blessing. I watch them eagerly read them at their birthday celebrations and then tuck them away. We are blessed as we write and deliver these words of love and acceptance.

The third part of the blessing is to attach a high value to the child. The first few elements lead up to the words of blessing themselves, the words of high value. To value something means to attach honor to it. The word "blessed" is used to show reverence or awe to an important person. These words of blessing need to convey the recognition that the person is valuable and has redeeming qualities. And these words need to be based on who that person is, not simply on his or her performance.

The fourth part of the blessing is intended to picture a special future. In the Old Testament, Isaac said to his son, Jacob, "May God give you of the dew of heaven, of the fatness of the earth . . . let people serve you, and nations bow down to you" (Genesis 27:28–29). We cannot predict another person's future with accuracy. However, we can encourage and help our children set meaningful goals. We can also convey to them that the gifts and character traits they have are attributes that God can both bless now and use in the future. With this fourth element of the blessing, children gain a sense of security in the present and grow in confidence to serve God and others in the future.

Parental Roles in Spiritual Formation

The last part of the family blessing is an act of commitment on the part of the person giving the blessing, as was instituted in the Old Testament. There is a responsibility that goes with giving the blessing. Your children will need to be reminded that they have been blessed. You need to know that God stands behind the words you have bestowed upon your children. You can rely upon the Lord to give you strength and perseverance to confirm and reaffirm your children's blessings. You have God's Word through the Scriptures as a guide, and the enduring power of the Holy Spirit.

As a children's pastor, I officiated the baby dedications that were held monthly in our church. In our particular setting and tradition, each family chose special guests to invite to the dedication service. Each family participating was encouraged to bring words of blessing or an item of significance to the ceremony. After the large group gathering, the families split into their own groups to bless their child. Many purchased a special candle that was lit for the first time at this ceremony and would be reignited on each subsequent birthday as the story of the child's dedication was told and retold.

Some families had "God boxes" made to hold all the items that had spiritual significance or meaning for their child. I remember one family who had a small trunk for each of their children so they could keep all the items they treasured from their childhood, their dedication candle, and books that were especially meaningful to them. These boxes were available to the children in their quiet times. When they couldn't sleep, they were allowed to pull out their boxes and hold and touch each item as they remembered the life events those items symbolized, over and over again. The children loved to touch, feel, and remember.

Another family held a blessing time in their home for their daughter who had just turned thirteen. Members of the community were invited to write special words for the girl that would be read at this gathering. How precious that time was as we surrounded her with our love and read her the blessings one by one. We finished our time together with blessing prayers. The girl was launched into the next stage of life by her family and her loving community. How beautiful and meaningful it was!

ADDITIONAL ROLES

Sacred Connector, Nurturer, and Bestower of Blessings are only a few of the roles you take on as a parent when cooperating with God in the spiritual formation of your children's hearts, souls, and minds. As parents, you are role models, whether you want to be or not. If children see and experience Christ in their parents, they are more likely to choose the path their Godly parents have set for them. Your actions will always win out over your words.

You can also choose to become an astute listener, observer, and prayer warrior in order to support, guide, and direct your children on the right path. I love the story of the nine-year-old boy who was soaking in the bathtub when he called out to his mother to come to him. The bathtub was his favorite thinking place. His mother could tell this was one of those serious times because of the thoughtful look on his face. Sure enough, he came out with a big important question—one that could really send a parent reeling. He said to her, "What if we don't have the story about God right?" His mother realized how serious and troubled he was about this possibility and immediately acknowledged her need inwardly for help. She gave her son a moment and then asked him to close his eyes and tell her what he saw. He looked and then began to tell her with a sense of awe and wonder. The whole universe had rolled out before him in his inner sight, and he knew there was a God even though he may not have the whole story right. She was able to comfort him with her prayerful listening and astute observation. It was indeed a crossroads moment for him, and she was able to meet him there with her quiet, confident presence.

One of the most glorious roles is that of reversal. The child leads the way on the path toward spiritual maturity and the adult journeys with them. In God's Kingdom on Earth, where we experience many paradoxes, this possibility is certainly one of them. And why not?! Christ continually invites us to come to the Kingdom as a child, humbly, exuberantly, full of questions, and fully present in the moments of everyday life. What a joy we, as parents, can experience as we walk with our children in the Kingdom of God on Earth and learn to love and enjoy Him abundantly. A beautiful young mother told me about her experiences walking in God's world and learning together with her four daughters:

> I often go on walks with the children. On our walks, we stop and look at nature. We notice how the veins on a leaf mirror the

branches of a tree and marvel at God's cleverness. We try to find heart shapes in the tree branches and laugh at God's humor. We go to the beach and remember that there are more stars in the sky than all of the grains of sand on the earth, and God created them all. We collect acorns and marvel that a mature oak tree drops 100,000 acorns in a season and only a few baby oaks grow from that. We wonder how God thought of feeding squirrels with acorns and leaving just enough to grow. The girls often come home and draw their image of God and the beauty they see in the natural world.

Stories help us see and understand a little more clearly. Judy Gattis Smith, an author and Christian educator, has written some parables that I use in my teaching. Which one of the following parables would you say fits the parenting style of this young mother?

1

I took a child's hand in mine. He and I were to talk together for a while. It was a great task that overcame me, so awful was the responsibility. I was to lead him to the Holy One. And so I talked to the little child only of the Holy One. I painted the sternness of Him, were the child to displease the Holy One. I spoke of the child's goodness as something that would appease His wrath. We walked under the tall trees. I said the Holy One had the power to send them crashing down, struck by thunderbolts. We walked in the sunshine, and I told him of the greatness of the Holy One who made the burning, blazing sun. And one twilight we met Him. The child hid behind me. He was afraid. He did not look up at the face so loving! He remembered the picture I had painted of Him. He did not take the Holy One's hand. I was between the child and the Holy One. I wondered why I had been so conscientious, so serious.

2

I took a little child's hand in mine. I was to lead him to the Holy One. I felt burdened with the multiplicity of the things I had to teach him. We did not ramble; we hastened from spot to spot. At one moment we compared the leaves of the different trees. At the next we were examining a bird's nest. While the child was questioning me about it, I hurried him away to catch a butterfly. Did he chance to fall asleep, I awakened him lest he should miss something I wished him to see. We spoke of the Holy One, oh yes, often and rapidly. I poured his ears full of all the stories he ought to know, often and rapidly. But we were interrupted by the wind blowing, of which we must speak, by the coming of the stars, which he must study, by the gurgling brook, which he must track to its source. And then in the twilight we met the Holy One. The child merely glanced at Him, and then his gaze wandered in a dozen different directions. The Holy One stretched out a hand. The child was not interested enough to take it. Feverish spots burned on his cheeks. He dropped exhausted to the ground and fell asleep. I was between the child and the Holy One. I wondered why I had taught him so many, many things.

3

I took a little child's hand to lead him to the Holy One. My heart was filled with gratitude for the glad privilege. We walked slowly. I suited my steps to the short steps of the child. We spoke of the things the child noticed. Sometimes it was one of the Holy One's birds. We watched it build its nest. We saw the eggs that were laid. We wondered later at the care it gave its young. Sometimes we picked up the Holy One's flowers and stroked their soft petals and admired the bright colors. Often we told stories of the Holy One. I told them to the child, and the child told them to me. We told them, the child and I, over and over again. Sometimes we stopped to rest, leaning against one of the Holy One's trees and letting the breezes cool our brows, never speaking. And then in the twilight we met the Holy One. The child's eyes shone! He put his hand into the Holy One's hand. I was for the moment forgotten . . . I was content.[1]

As you make sacred connections, nurture and bless your children, you are helping them seek answers to life's greatest questions for themselves as well as for yourself: who am I, who made me, and what am I here for? Living and growing with your children is the great equalizer. You will be equally enriched in body, soul, mind, and heart.

QUESTIONS TO CONSIDER

1. If you were the child, which story would you rather be a part of?
2. How do you feel about each of the roles discussed in this chapter?

---

1. Smith, *Spiritual Development Through Sight, Smell, Taste, and Touch*, 77–78.

Parental Roles in Spiritual Formation

3. Which one are you most comfortable with?
4. Which one will be your greatest challenge?
5. How will you go about growing in that role?
6. When and how were you blessed?
7. Who were the significant role models that influenced your life?
8. How did they do it?
9. What are the areas of growth in your relationship with God?
10. As you become a student of your child, what are you noticing?
11. What gives you hope?

4

How Spirituality Looks in Children

Now faith is the assurance of things hoped for, the conviction of things not seen. For by it the men of old gained approval. By faith we understand that the worlds were prepared by the word of God, so that what is seen was not made out of things which are visible.

—HEBREWS 11:1–3

IN ORDER TO RECOGNIZE a spiritual experience in your child, you need to have some understanding of what it might look like. And to help you understand what it might look like, you need a basic understanding of the terms *faith, religion,* and *spirituality*. Most likely you have defined these words based on your own experiences. But it will be helpful in the coming chapters to understand what I mean when I use them, even if you don't agree with my definitions.

Faith, religion, and *spirituality* are often used interchangeably, which can result in some confusion. To help you understand their distinctions, I have chosen definitions that I believe best fit the spiritual formation model that will be explained in chapter 6.

FAITH

What is faith? I define faith as a belief and trust in God so strong that it becomes the inner force that propels a person to venture into the unknown of life in a trusting and confident way, resulting in spiritual growth and the development of a strong character. We know that faith can never be tested in a laboratory. Even for the youngest child, faith can be described as a strong sense of being held in the care and the love of God. Children and parents never lose their need for that kind of love.

Sophia Cavalletti, the author of *Religious Potential of the Child*, makes an interesting statement about the relationship between this type of faith, or trust in God, and the resulting spiritual growth and development of character. She says that "the relationship between orientation and action is like a plant and its fruit; there are living fruits only if the plant is healthy and rooted deeply in the earth. Actions are the manifold expressions of the global orientation of the person."[1] Since children follow their parents lead, it is important for parents to be living examples of their values and beliefs on a daily basis. The children will reflect this in their own spiritual growth. Our actions, as parents and spiritual beings, always speak louder than our words and reveal our true character.

A mother of a thirteen-year-old girl shared this story with me about the development of character in her daughter:

> When Heidi was small, we got her a short broom. When I swept, she swept. We sang and laughed and had a great time. Later, when God began to waken my heart to Him, I openly gave my sin and pain to Jesus. Then, when Heidi became aware of her sin, she too openly gave her sin and pain to Jesus. The result of her willingness to give her sin to Jesus is a continuous freedom toward her true self. As Jesus takes her sin, her faith grows, and as he takes her sin and fills her with His love and His plan for her, her character becomes stronger. As her mother, I stand in awe of her selflessness, her love for her little sisters, and her servant's heart among many other wonderful attributes. These are God's gifts to her because of her obedience. She is free!

She lovingly followed her mother's example as she swept, sang, and laughed. She also experienced her mother's relationship with God and developed her own. Because of that, Heidi's character began to consistently reflect her relationship with God, free from guilt and shame. She knows who she is: one of God's beloved daughters. You could see this relationship in the way she carried herself. She moved freely, able to stand straight and tall in who she is. She is full of love for her siblings and parents as well as others in her world. She lives an authentic life everywhere she goes. It is beautiful to see.

How does that essential trust in God grow? As very young children, we all have a fundamental need to be loved in a profound way. Only when this need is met does a basic trust emerge that enables us to live in har-

---

1. Cavalletti, *Religious Potential of the Child*, 152.

mony with the world. When we know God loves us unconditionally, we develop a trusting faith and a loving relationship with Him. What follows then around six years of age can be defined as morality: a response to God's love, or our reaction to our encounters with Him. Falling in love with God enables us to move toward loving ourselves as God loves us and then sharing that love with others. The development of that morality shows itself in a child's relationships with others.

RELIGION

Emile Durkheim, who is considered to be the father of sociology and is the author of *The Elementary Forms of Religion,* defined religion this way: "It is a unified system of beliefs and practices relative to sacred things."[2] I agree with him but have a few more thoughts of my own. I define religion as a system of beliefs that provide the framework and structure in which a person's faith is taught and lived out with others of like beliefs, cultures, and traditions. Peter Kreeft, who wrote *The Handbook of Christian Apologetics,* says, "Science only asks what and how, philosophy asks why, but it is religion that asks who."[3]

In *The Dance with God,* Walter Wangerin discusses what happens when a child experiences both faith and religion. He asks whether fixed doctrines, which characterize a lot of religious experience, can stifle the child's first experiences of God. He believes they won't if the child's experience provides room for change and growth. As long as the child has the freedom to "dance with God" in this relationship, he or she can change and grow.

Talking with your children about their encounters with God validates or affirms their experiences. It gives the experience the right to endure, praises your children for their relationship with God, and lets them know that they are worshipping the same God you are. Then the child can speak about his or her faith out loud and commit to a lifelong relationship with God. This is very much like a vow. Wangerin says, "It is the most committed way to say, 'I love you'. Not only, has the child come to love the God that now he/she can name; not only has he/she experienced the love; but is allowed language—his/her own language—to confirm it."[4]

2. Hexham, *A Concise Dictionary of Religion,* 187.
3. Komp, *A Window to Heaven,* 53.
4. Wangerin, *The Orphean Passages,* 25.

SPIRITUALITY

The word *spirituality* has become popular in American culture today and is confusing for many. According to the *Concise Dictionary of Religion*, "many religious traditions teach that in addition to our bodies the human person has a spirit or soul which lives within the body, giving it life and everything that is distinctly human. It is this aspect of the person which is believed to relate to God and the religious realm."[5]

I believe that children come into this world with an imprint of their spiritual life on their being. They are capable of relating to God in ways we don't see or can't understand. In fact, a child is the most pure form of the image of God we will ever know in this life, as I stated in an earlier chapter. Children are created with an ability to know and relate to the God who made them. They are spiritual beings in a human body. That is a crucial piece of information to digest if any of the rest of this book is going to make sense and be useful to you. Your child's whole life will be spent trying to reconcile his or her spiritual being and humanity to the way that God intended it. Sin obstructs their light and robs them of the intimacy of the relationship they once enjoyed but are beginning to forget.

As children mature in age, they need to relearn how to be, first and foremost, a spiritual person, rightly related to the God who made them and the world. Just like adults, children must practice their spirituality in order to keep it fresh and alive. But instead of trying to figure it out on their own, children will most likely wonder about it and look for the source.

An interesting article in the August 13, 1993, issue of the *St. Paul Pioneer Press* says, "The version of God that children embrace often has nothing to do with that of their parents. Children raised without religious instruction, or without parents who believe, discover God in the playground and at nursery school, absorb Him by way of baby sitters and friends, have their awareness of Him reinforced by movies, television and the profanity of the street. Martha Fay, in the book *Do Children Need Religion*, writes, "He is, indeed, everywhere, and parents who suggest otherwise are often surprised by the intensity with which their children insist on God's reality.""[6]

---

5. Hexham, *Concise Dictionary of Religion*, 207.
6. Landers, "What Kids Ask (and Know) about God," *St. Paul Pioneer Press*, 8G.

How Spirituality Looks in Children

SPIRITUALITY IN CHILDREN

One of my favorite authors and teachers, Sophia Cavaletti, makes some assumptions about children's spirituality. She wholeheartedly believes that children experience God and has great respect for their God encounters. In her book, *Religious Potential of the Child,* she indicates four basic assumptions about the spiritual lives of children.

It is the relationship itself that is important rather than the form. God cannot be fully caught by the logic structures of any age or stage. A child's spiritual potential is a global experience in two ways. It touches the child's total being and is not the function of some isolated psychic or physical mechanism. Spirituality is also "natural," Cavalletti says, so it is essential to what defines being human regardless of where the child is born on the globe.

Human beings are not fully developing unless their spiritual potential is stimulated and growing. Spiritual potential is not a matter of willed commitment, intellectual reasoning, or political force. It is systemic to human health.

The religious language Cavalletti works with, the Judeo-Christian tradition, is a language that is very powerful as an agent to describe, evoke, and express the multidimensional aspects of a child's experience of God.[7]

The potential for spirituality is genetically wired within every child. It is stimulated in a primary way by God and given content and shape from one's culture. The developing relationship with God needs to be strong enough to restrain the culture from choking off the budding new life and future spiritual growth. If the culture is stronger than the relationship, the result would weaken the developing faith and trust and slow its growth. It is similar to what happens to a child's physical development if a bone is broken on the growth plate. It can slow down or inhibit the growth of the bone.

If we truly believe that children are created in God's image and come as light bearers into this world, we will not find this difficult to accept. Psalm 139:13–16 paints a beautiful picture of this:

> For though didst form my inward parts; Thou didst weave me in my mother's womb. I will give thanks to Thee, for I am fearfully and wonderfully made; Wonderful are Thy works, and my soul

---

7. Cavalletti, *Religious Potential of the Child,* 9.

knows it very well. My frame was not hidden from Thee, when I was made in secret, and skillfully wrought in the depths of the earth. Thine eyes have seen my unformed substance; and in Thy book they were all written, the days that were ordained for me, when as yet there was not one of them.

EVIDENCE OF SPIRITUALITY IN CHILDREN

What does spiritual potential, in terms of an experience that your child might have and that can be observed by outsiders, look like?

1. The experience of the child is spontaneous rather than a response to an adult's prompting. You can't make it happen for your child. It is between your child and God alone.
2. The experience is complex. It involves feelings, thoughts, and moral action, although moral consciousness is not expected until approximately age six.
3. The experience is not limited to cultural conditioning.
4. The experience is deep and multidimensional rather than a singular function like an auditory or visual memory. It involves the heart and mind.
5. The experience produces joy.
6. The experience causes prayers of praise or thanksgiving to flow from the child.[8]

Any one or combination of these experiences would indicate a response to God, an awareness of Him in ways we, as adults, find more difficult to experience and express.

RELATIONSHIP BETWEEN A RELIGIOUS SYSTEM AND SPIRITUALITY

What is the relationship between a religious system, then, and the development of spirituality? A young mother of a six-year-old boy explained her view to me: "Religion is a framework within which we have an opportunity to develop our spirituality. But you can be spiritual without being religious." I believe all humans are spiritual but have a choice about

---

8. Cavalletti, *Religious Potential of the Child,* 10.

How Spirituality Looks in Children

whether they choose a religious system in which to function and develop their theology or not. A community that fosters and supports the spiritual growth of children and their parents will produce stronger and more mature spirituality that is lived out in their daily lives.

Dr. Robert Coles, the author of *The Spiritual Life of Children,* also has something to say about the combination and progression from a religious system to the development of spirituality:

> Religions are known, of course, for their insistence on upholding various moral principles and standards, for the reinforcement they offer to their adherents' consciousness and to the culture of various nations. But less evident are the strategies boys and girls devise to accommodate a secular and familial morality, on the one hand, and the religious morality they hear espoused in churches, mosques, and synagogues. The task for these boys and girls is to weave together a particular version of a morality both personal and yet tied to a religious tradition, and the essence of the spiritual life is to ponder their moral successes and failures and, consequently their prospects as human beings who will some day die.[9]

In conclusion, I believe children are all born with a genetically imprinted desire to know who they are, how they came to be, and where they are going. They have a spiritual capacity to experience and know God and develop a trust and confidence in His love and care for them. They experience pure presence in the moment, abundant joy that is the natural outcome of presence, and later on, the development of an awareness of others. They were created to enjoy Him and to tell Him so. You, as the parent, and the community of people you have chosen that subscribe to the same religious beliefs and have experienced God themselves can nurture your child's spiritual formation and growth. Furthermore, if we all pay attention to the spiritual lives of our children, we might learn more about the roots of our own spiritual well being.

QUESTIONS TO CONSIDER

1. What early spiritual experiences can you recall?
2. What feelings are associated with those recollections?
3. What do you remember of your early religious experiences?

---

9. Coles, *The Spiritual Life of Children,* 115.

4. What sensory memories of those experiences do you have?
5. How might these memories affect your choice of community in which to raise your own children?
6. If you are involved in a faith community now, how respectful is it of people in all stages of life, including babies and the elderly?
7. How does your faith community view children's spirituality?
8. What is the role of nurture in the culture of your faith community?

5

The Formation of Spiritual and Religious Language

Since my youth, O God, you have taught me, and to this day, I declare your marvelous deeds. Even when I am old and gray, do not forsake me, O God till I declare your power to the next generation.

—Psalm 71:17–18

In order for childhood faith to stick, children must encounter the living God through their own experiences. They must know He is alive and at work in their world. If a child has only been told stories about someone else's experiences, even if they are Bible stories, chances are slim that the child will continue to follow the path set by his or her parents. And this happens quite early: By the time they are ten, most children have reached the stage where logic and reason take precedence, and matters of the heart become more difficult for them to experience. But if children have already been encouraged to develop a relationship with God and if they have the language to talk about their experiences, their heart will remain sensitive and responsive. Their minds may be bent toward logic, but their hearts can still connect with the living God.

Obtaining a spiritual and religious language requires help from someone who is willing and able to name the child's experiences with God. What comes from those moments of simple and basic understanding can then be catalogued in the child's mind and heart for future reference.

As has been stated in previous chapters, children come into this world having been formed by God's hand. They retain an imprint of Him on their lives. There is a kind of memory we cannot understand with our finite minds. He places within children a desire to know who made them. The veil between the spiritual world and the physical one is very thin for young children, enabling them to see and experience what adults often miss. For instance, many children see angels or even evil beings around them that adults can't see. They hear things we don't hear.

I had a conversation with a mother who told me her son had recently asked her to identify a tall man he saw in the hallway of their home. She looked but didn't see anyone standing there. Her boy insisted that he saw a man. His mother asked him if he felt the man was good or evil. The boy told her he had a good feeling. She then invited her son to pray with her. She asked God, in the name of Jesus, to take the man away if he was not from God. The boy, with much excitement, told her that now there were more of them. She called them angels. The mother and son were both filled with great peace. Even though the mother could not see what he saw, she validated his sighting.

NAMING OF SPIRITUAL EXPERIENCES

Just as children need help naming new things and ideas they discover in their everyday lives, children will not know what they are seeing or hearing in a spiritual experience unless an adult names it for them. And in order to name it for them, the adult must accept that the child sees something he or she can't see or hear. Sometimes it takes a while to attune one's ear to hear what a child is saying in order to respond appropriately.

In the Old Testament, young Samuel and Eli, the priest, have a "middle of the night" experience. As the story goes, Samuel awakens during the night by a voice calling his name. Not knowing where the voice is coming from, Samuel is scared and runs to Eli to tell him what he heard. Eli comforts Samuel and sends him back to bed. When the voice calls for Samuel a few more times, Eli finally realizes that the boy is hearing the voice of God but Samuel doesn't know God's voice yet. So, Eli names the experience for Samuel and tells him how to respond when he hears the voice again. Samuel was then able to recognize God's voice and eventually went on to become one of the greatest and most important prophets of God.

What a great example of how naming experiences gives children a language to use and validates their encounters with God. When children are able to share their experiences with us using the spiritual language they have learned, we get to enjoy and partake in wonderful moments of awe and wonder together. Furthermore, since they haven't fallen into the pattern of using the old clichés common among an adult's spiritual language, a child's spiritual language is typically fresh and new, offering a perspective we may have never thought of before.

NAMING OF RELIGIOUS EXPERIENCES

Developing a child's religious language to name the experiences and beliefs of his or her community is important as well. Language that is specific to the practices and rituals children experience will become a part of their everyday religious language. The words peculiar to their culture will also affect their religious language. For example, liturgical language has meaning for children raised in liturgical churches, while charismatic language becomes part of the vocabulary of those raised in a charismatic church. Religious language is not necessarily spiritual, but it does help children name their experiences and beliefs as part of the community of faith and culture.

A young mother told me about what her family called the "God bowl," which she fills with water every day. The bowl symbolizes for them the filling by the Holy Spirit of all the empty places in their spirits and souls. Her family gathers around the bowl to read Bible stories. Religious language and rituals they have developed are used during the experience, followed by a quiet period in order to let God fill their hearts. Several times after doing this, her girls have been able to express how full of God's love they feel in the language they have been taught.

Both a spiritual language and a religious language are important from the very beginning. When God is called upon or named in everyday life, the child grows up naming Him also. It also is important for children to speak the same language as the community of faith they belong to. However, religious language is not the ultimate goal; it only names their particular beliefs and is not sacred in and of itself.

In faith communities, the particular words and phrases used during times together become absorbed and used outside of community gatherings. The potential danger with religious language is if a child's understanding of the language is not stretched beyond the comfort of his or her community. It's important to explain that other communities have different ways of speaking about their faith. I have heard children be deeply critical of other children whose religious language differs from theirs. It is easy for them—and for us—to fall into the trap of thinking our way is the only way of speaking about faith.

It takes time and effort to be able to decode another person's story, and even more time and effort to really understand it. Even harder yet is a parent's job of helping a child learn tolerance for another person's faith stories. Speaking a common language in their own faith community does not mean it is the only way to describe and talk about experiences with God.

Dr. Robert Coles, author of *The Spiritual Life of Children,* interviewed hundreds of children with different cultural, social, and racial differences and found strong similarities in their descriptions of experiences with God, even though their religious experiences differed greatly. God makes Himself known to all people, regardless of culture or geographic location, and what is essential is experienced across those borders and experiences.

In summary, it is important to help children develop language for both types of expression: spiritual and religious. They need a healthy balance of both in order to describe their experiences of God within and outside of their community of faith.

LAYERS OF SPIRITUAL AND RELIGIOUS LANGUAGE

Jerome Berryman, author of *Godly Play,* has a unique way of looking at the development of spiritual and religious languages. To represent them, he uses five concentric circles layered inside each other. Silence, overflowing silence, sacred story, law codes and proverbs and theology make up his circular representation for our spiritual and religious language. In healthy development, a person moves from the inner circle to the outer ring and back again; the outer ring is not the ending place. The ability to express one's theology does not result in a transformed life by itself. Instead, in our life's journeys we all need to dip back into the stories of faith and the moments of wonder and awe to keep us fresh and vibrant in our relationship to God.

Here is Berryman's visual representation of the development of spiritual and religious language:[1]

---

1. Berryman, *Godly Play: A Way of Religious Education,* 152.

The Formation of Spiritual and Religious Language

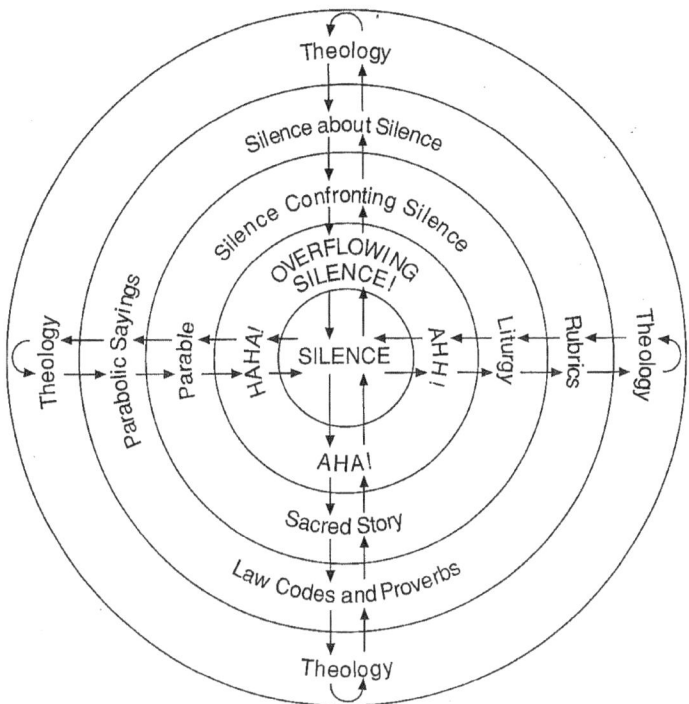

Silence

The center circle represents the place of our beginnings of language. Silence, which is used from conception into infancy, is our first language. At first this was a strange concept to me. How can silence be a language? Eventually I came to understand that silence does not mean absence of thought or understanding. It simply is a way of being attentive to all that comes into a person's awareness. When a person is attentive in the moment, the absorption of an experience happens.

Communication is part listening, part being attentive and receptive, and part responding. When you don't have words blocking your ability to listen, you can truly be attentive to what is happening in your spirit and the world around you. You need to be still in order to become aware of the presence of God in your life and the world. Out of this attentiveness come responses of praise, wonder, and awe—all characteristics of very young children.

The famous educator Maria Montessori describes ages and stages of development in terms of sensitivities. Infancy is a sensitive period for language. Infants learn the language of the family and culture that they are a part of, and at no other time will they be so attuned to the language of wonder, awe, and praise. This is the language of the spiritual realm from which infants have so recently come.

Silence is actually pre-language. No words are required, and the result is a form of worship. The type of silence I am talking about is not the silence imposed from outside. Instead, the silence that infants experience is something that comes from within them. It brings rest to the body and memory to the spirit. It is the wordless language of experience. Psalm 81 refers to the infant who is capable of praise and worship.

While infancy may be the sensitive period for this kind of language, we never stop needing the same kind of silence and all that it brings with it. For all of us, in moments of stillness, God's reality breaks in on us. God's presence leaves us filled with wonder and awe. It is expressed by *aahs, ahas,* and *ha-has*. Young children live in a world of wonder as they discover and experience so much in such a short period of time. They know a form of perfect worship.

My four-year-old grandson and I were playing outside one day. As usual, he was fascinated with the ants' activity on the sidewalk. He watched and studied them for the longest time. I simply sat by him while he entered the world of the ant. Per his instruction, we left the ants to lie on our backs and look at the sky and clouds. There was very little conversation as we looked at the sky. It was a beautiful day with a lot of fluffy clouds in the sky. A plane flew overhead. He studied that plane as it passed over us. I wasn't sure why it caught his attention because it was not a new experience for him. After a short time, the answer became clear. He was having an *aah* experience. I could tell by the change in his demeanor. He was feeling awe and wonder!

Eventually he broke the silence by telling me what he had been thinking in his reverie. He deduced that we must look like ants to those people in the airplane and to God. He was absolutely awestruck at the thought that we were so tiny in comparison to what he knew of the universe. He had no words to really communicate the magnitude of what he had discovered and felt. The whole experience felt sacred to me, and I knew I needed to just listen and leave it alone for him to ponder.

The Formation of Spiritual and Religious Language

A little older child often has more words to describe experiences of God. A teacher of six-year-olds asked her group whether any of them had ever felt that God was with them. One child answered affirmatively. When asked specifically about the occasion, she told the teacher she had felt God when she was sick. The teacher knew that the child had been hospitalized with a high fever when she was four. She wondered whether the child was merely repeating words she had heard from her parents. When the teacher asked the girl's mother about it, however, the mother said neither she nor her husband had ever discussed anything of that nature with their daughter. The teacher was not surprised. The child had spoken with such a calm manner and exhibited wisdom beyond her years. In her solitude she had been drawn into silence and God's presence.

Jean Gasso Fitzpatrick, who wrote *Something More: Nurturing Your Child's Spiritual Growth,* says, "Without any instruction at all, even the youngest child can discover the presence that speaks in the absence of noise."[2] I believe this with all my heart because I have seen and experienced it.

Layer of Liturgy: Language of the People

Liturgy provides the particular form or rituals used in public worship by a faith community. There is no theologizing in this layer of language. The use of the imagination and reflection while stories are told or read is of utmost importance. Young preschoolers and children in the first few grades of school get deeply involved in stories of faith. These accounts meet both the needs of their emotions and their intellect, the need for love and protection, and the need for justice and fairness. When this happens, God ministers to their deep needs. Catherine Stonehouse, the author of *Joining Children on the Spiritual Journey,* shared a story about her work with a third-grade boy that illustrates this well.

Jonathan's teenage sister, Angela, had died of cancer, and his grief had been great. As I prepared to tell the Good Shepherd parable for the children, I prayed that Jonathan would be able to meet the Good Shepherd in the parable and be comforted. For three Sundays I told the Good Shepherd story, expanding it to include the story of the lost sheep and finally of the ordinary shepherd who ran away when the wolf came. Each week Jonathan listened intently to the story, but during response

---

2. Fitzpatrick, *Something More: Nurturing Your Child's Spiritual Growth,* 147.

time he happily made whatever his friend John was making—items that had nothing to do with the story.

On the fourth Sunday I presented the story of the Light. "Once there was someone who said such wonderful things and did such amazing things that the people began to follow him. But they didn't know who he was. So they just had to ask him, and he said, 'I am the Light.'" I lit the Christ candle, and we enjoyed the light. "Those who love the Light," I told the children, "take their light from the Light." Then I proceeded to light a small candle for each child, holding up their candle, looking them in the eyes, and saying their name, "Emily, this is your light. . . ."

It was not a good morning. Several children were distracted, making comments to get the attention of others, but I plowed ahead, saying, "See how the light has spread? So many have received their light from the Light, and yet the Light is still the same." I lit Jonathan's candle and turned to speak to him when he blurted out, "That's Angela's light." "Yes," I responded, "Angela did take her light from the Light, and now Angela is with the Light forever, and this is Jonathan's light."

At the close of the story I let Jonathan be the first to choose his work, thinking that he might want to use the materials from the story of the Light. Instead, he took the Good Shepherd parable box and spent the rest of the hour immersed in the story of the Good Shepherd. The following Sunday Jonathan again chose to work with the Good Shepherd story. One of the adult workers went over to Jonathan and began asking him questions about the story. In just a few minutes Jonathan put the materials away.

Was he finished with the story, or had his time with the Good Shepherd been interrupted because he could not verbalize what he knew and felt of the Shepherd as he simply entered the story? I think the latter was true, since the next Sunday he again returned to work with the Good Shepherd. Somehow, the symbol of the Light connected with Jonathan's deep inner feelings and brought into his consciousness Angela and his grief. He now knew where to go with his pain. He went to the Good Shepherd and spent time with him in the story. Maybe someday Jonathan will be able to tell me what went on between him and the Shepherd on those three Sunday mornings, but as a third grader he could only be with the Shepherd.[3]

---

[3] Stonehouse, *Joining Children on the Spiritual Journey: Nurturing the Life of Faith*, 179–80.

The Formation of Spiritual and Religious Language

Children do not process logically or even verbally very often. But as they move through the story or symbols, they can expect to meet God, who will lead them to the discoveries and meaning they need. Parables continue to be excellent stories for them. Children also need deep experiential involvement in rituals. In the story of Jonathan's journey, the lighting of a small candle for their quiet time was an example of a meaningful ritual.

Layer of Rubric, Law Codes, and Parabolic Sayings

Children in the later grades of elementary school and preteens can begin to understand the meaning of liturgy, parables, and symbols. This age group can analyze sacred stories and use abstract word symbols. The meaning and application of biblical texts makes sense to them. They are able to think logically and abstractly. If a child has already had experiences of God, the study of narratives as well as the law codes can reinforce what they have already experienced. A solid faith begins to emerge from their foundation of trust, which can take them through the hard knocks that may come during adolescence and adulthood.

If a child does not have that foundation, he or she will need a conversion experience to bring the child back to God. Then He will transform the child's heart. A solid foundation of trust results in faith that leads to a basis for hope in the midst of a troubled world. Brennan Manning, a former priest who wrote *Ruthless Trust*, says that if trust does not develop first during the sensitive period, the order for faith development is reversed. Instead of trust coming first (from birth to two years old) it comes last. The new order is faith, hope, and then, finally, trust. The new order is completely dependent on a gift of grace from God. Only then can transformation take place in the heart and soul of a person.

James Fowler, the author of *Stages of Faith and Religious Development*, says that conversion is not the goal or even the end of the journey. The development of faith continues throughout our entire lives. As we move steadily along through the journey of life, we are changing. The changes that occur prepare us for the next developmental phase. We will have what we need for the next part of our journey of faith.

Theology Layer

Theology is a language about God. Everything we have learned about God through experience and study of Scripture is boiled down to a system that describes what God is like, how God acts, who we are, and how we relate to others and the world. The following story is about an eight-year-old boy whose school assignment was to explain God—an enormous task for anyone, much less a child. Here's his response, which was circulated on the Internet by the boy's teacher:

> One of God's main jobs is making people. He makes them to replace the ones that die, so there will be enough people to take care of things on earth. He doesn't make grownups, just babies. I think because they are smaller and easier to make. That way he doesn't have to take up his valuable time teaching them to talk and walk. He can just leave that to mothers and fathers.
>
> God's second most important job is listening to prayers. An awful lot of this goes on, since some people, like preachers and things, pray at times beside bedtime. God doesn't have time to listen to the radio or TV because of this. Because he hears everything, there must be a terrible lot of noise in his ears, unless he has thought of a way to turn it off.
>
> God sees everything and hears everything and is everywhere, which keeps Him pretty busy. So you shouldn't go wasting his time by going over your mom and dad's head asking for something they said you couldn't have.
>
> Atheists are people who don't believe in God. I don't think there are any in Chula Vista. At least there aren't any who come to our church.
>
> Jesus is God's son. He used to do all the hard work, like walking on water and performing miracles and trying to teach the people who didn't want to learn about God. They finally got tired of him preaching to them and they crucified him. But he was good and kind, like his father, and he told his father that they didn't know what they were doing and to forgive them and God said OK.
>
> His dad (God) appreciated everything that he had done and all his hard work on earth. So he told him he didn't have to go out on the road anymore. He could stay in heaven. So he did. And now he helps his dad out by listening to prayers and seeing things that are important for God to take care of and which ones he can take care of himself without having to bother God. Like a secretary, only more important.

The Formation of Spiritual and Religious Language

> You can pray anytime you want and they are sure to help you because they got it worked out so one of them is on duty all the time. You should always go to church on Sunday because it makes God happy, and if there's anybody you want to make happy, it's God.
>
> Don't skip church to do something you think will be more fun like going to the beach. This is wrong. And, besides, the sun doesn't come out at the beach until noon anyway.
>
> If you don't believe in God, besides being an atheist, you will be very lonely, because your parents can't go everywhere with you, like to camp, but God can. It is good to know He's around you when you're scared, in the dark, or when you can't swim and you get thrown into real deep water by big kids.
>
> But . . . you shouldn't just always think of what God can do for you. I figure God put me here and he can take me back anytime he pleases.
>
> And . . . that's why I believe in God.

This boy's theology may differ from yours, but it is his at this stage of his life. Give him this same assignment in another ten years and the answer will likely change considerably. Often as adults we think we have arrived when we have a solid theology. We attach it to a framework in which a person's faith is taught and lived out with others of like beliefs, culture, and traditions. We have all the words we need to describe and understand what we believe. It is so easy to forget to move back into the center, back to the core where silence is the language. It is there that we relive the stories and experience God in a new way with a sense of wonder and awe.

At times, God reveals Himself to each of us in a way that gets our attention very quickly. In a childlike moment of clarity, I experienced something that felt miraculous to me. A friend and I were taking a stroll on Laguna Beach in California. Upon walking into the beach area, I found myself drawn to the tiered landscaping at the entrance to the beach. None of the flowers were open. In light of that, my next action makes no earthly sense. I leaned over a single flower that was tightly closed, cupped my hands beneath it without touching the bud, and leaned down to smell it. As I moved toward the flower, the bud opened completely in front of my eyes. It was as if I was watching time-lapsed photography of the opening of a flower. My friend was watching this miraculous unfolding from over my shoulder. Neither one of us said a word for while. We knew it was a silent sacred moment and did not want to spoil it with words.

We walked and began to wonder out loud together about its possible meaning. We both experienced in the silence the *aah* . . . and continued to experience the *aha* . . . as God continued to reveal its meaning to us.

It continues to unfold anew little by little. It reminds me of the words of the hymn by Henry Van Dyke to Beethoven's melody, *Joyful, joyful, we adore Thee / Hearts unfold like flowers before Thee / Open to the Son above.* He allowed me to see the closed bud reveal its inner beauty as it opened. The sunlight shown directly on the purple interior, which had a gold cross in the middle of it. It was clear pictures to me of the hearts of children, ready to receive God's light and reflect His beauty to all who can see.

There was silence and a beauty to behold. There was no need for a theological word. Speaking at the time would have destroyed or shortened the life of the sacred moment. A child would have experienced the same sense of awe and wonder upon seeing the flower open as we did. We have developmental differences that affect how we see and hear, but this story provides common ground for all to experience God. There is a natural progression here. We can enjoy God, receive God's love, love Him back, follow Him, and begin to see opportunities to serve Him by helping those around us.

All of us need to go back to that utterly quiet place in order to sit in God's presence and enjoy Him, always listening for His voice that sounds like "a whisper across my heart and out my mind," as a five-year-old boy who attended our church discovered. It is one of the ways we come to God like children again. It is one of the ways of wisdom that has the power to shape our children and transform us.

QUESTIONS TO CONSIDER

1. Where are you most comfortable in the layer of languages, as illustrated by Jerome Berryman?
2. Which layer is most foreign to your experience?
3. What new steps will you take as you seek to help your child acquire both a spiritual and religious language?
4. What layers of language do you find your children using?
5. What are the words of your particular religious system?

The Formation of Spiritual and Religious Language

6. What words come directly from your culture?
7. What words do you frequently use to describe your experiences of God?
8. What words do you hear your children use?
9. What do you suppose happens to a child's understanding and experience of God when the only naming of Him comes in the form of swearing and curses?

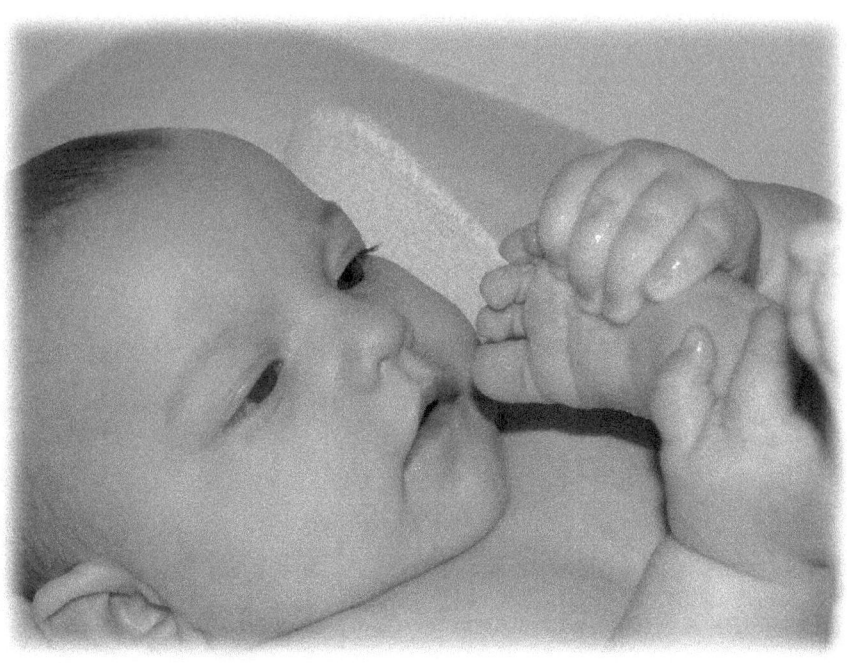

6

The Role of Child Development in Spiritual Formation

Like an open book, you watched me grow from conception to birth; all the stages of my life were spread out before you, the days of my life all prepared before I'd even lived one day.

—Psalm 139:16[1]

In chapter 5 I wrote about the transition from the silent language of children's first years to the formation of their concepts about God into a theology. This pattern of language is only one facet of development. In this chapter I will lay a foundation for understanding how the development of physical, social-emotional, cognitive, and moral development affects your child's spiritual formation.

CHILD DEVELOPMENT

All children develop in very specific and predictable patterns. In fact, developmental theorists have categorized and detailed the various stages of development that take a person from birth to death. How does understanding child development help us reach the ultimate goal of spiritual formation, which is to see Christ formed in us and in our children? To answer that question, I had to first ask these:

- Are child development and spiritual formation the same thing with different names?
- If not, are they parallel paths one takes toward maturity?
- Is there an integrated understanding of the two?

---

1. Peterson, *The Message*, Psalm 139:16.

During my studies of human development and, even more specifically, child development, I discovered that a significant amount of research existed about physical, social-emotional, cognitive, and moral development. However, there was little information about where spiritual development fit in. I even began to wonder if there was such a thing. This question led me to look closely at Sunday school curriculums and materials for parents to use at home. What I found was that these resources consistently addressed children's needs for knowledge and understanding in two basic ways:

- By giving an abundance of information about God and Jesus or a religious system's beliefs
- By attempting to meet social-emotional needs by modeling God's love to children

Both were important, but the picture felt incomplete to me. I have known too many adults who have grown up with all kinds of information about God and religion but never learned to recognize encounters with the living God. Nor had they developed a real relationship with Him. My own experience of profound need, dependence, and trust spoke to the fact that there was more to life than the acquisition of knowledge and good self-esteem. Hence, I began to listen to and watch children to see what they were experiencing, asking, and seeming to understand. I started realizing that the spiritual part of a child develops in chorus with the body and intellect but occasionally jumps ahead of cognitive ability with deep understanding.

Instead of looking at spirituality apart from the development of the whole child, I believe that all areas of development are linked together. And each area is a doorway for a child to develop a relationship with God and an awareness of Him at work in their lives. The following diagram explains how all areas of development work together to aid in a child's relationship with God and others.

The Role of Child Development in Spiritual Formation

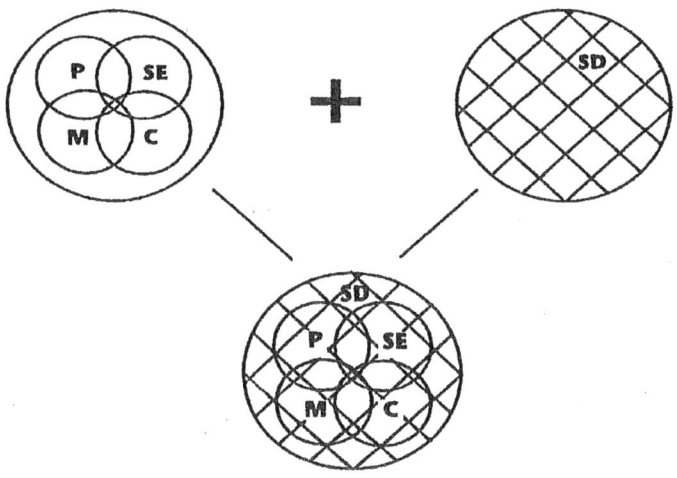

Physical Development

The physical development area, or doorway, is labeled *P* on the diagram. Beginning in the womb, a child physically grows and develops according to uniquely prescribed patterns that are both similar and different from other children.

A recent PBS special documenting the life of an unborn child through the use of an implanted camera in the uterus of a mother shows that babies dream while in the uterus. One has to wonder how they dream without having physical life experiences and language. Where does the material for a dream come from? I believe babies carry memory into this physical life from their beginnings with God. They have had a taste of life in God's kingdom and will spend the rest of their lives on earth craving it.

While in the womb, a baby can hear the mother's voice and heartbeat. Recent studies have shown that in the seventh month of pregnancy, the unborn infant will move its mouth when the mother speaks. At the same time the mother is speaking, the baby is trying to make the same sounds. How amazing that is!

Many parents have found that a song sung repeatedly to an unborn child elicits a visible response in them when it is sung after birth. Such songs bring comfort and command attention from them. If the rhythm is in sync with the mother's heartbeat, it has proven to be even more memorable and soothing to the child. For some children, their womb song remains one of their favorites for life, even if they don't know why. It should go without saying that the song you choose should be soothing and calming without busy rhythms or jarring sounds.

After birth, the same song can be played or sung at times when the baby needs to be soothed. It is familiar and brings back memories of the warm comfort inside the womb. If the words are scriptural or full of expressions of love, it can impact a child's heart even though they may not understand it intellectually. The heart's power to receive is not limited by a small vocabulary and underdeveloped intellect.

During the first year of a child's life, he or she is physically developing at such a fast pace. Every few weeks, there are new things happening in their physical development. They become more and more acclimated to their earthly environments, but they have not forgotten their earliest beginnings as image bearers of God. In a previous chapter I shared the story of the three-year-old girl who wanted to ask her baby brother if he could tell her about God because she was starting to forget Him.

Just as newborns remember their mother's voice after birth, so do children respond to God's voice. But the physical separation that happens at birth makes it necessary for babies to connect the voice they heard in utero to the mother's sound and touch in a new way. The same principle applies to life with God. After being born, a child will see, hear, touch, and taste through a thin veil that separates this world from the unseen world of God. To sustain this connection, names will have to be attached to experiences with God.

The famous Italian educator Maria Montessori and Sophia Cavalletti, an Italian professor of theology and developer of the Good Shepherd Model of Religious Education, believe there are periods of time in the very early years of your child's life that are optimum for learning or grasping a particular truth. Catherine Stonehouse, who wrote *Joining Children on The Spiritual Journey,* says:

> At various ages children become aware of different realities of the gospel. There will never be a time in life when the person can grasp the truth as easily as in the sensitive period. Realities comprehended during these prime times for learning live on within, sustaining us.

The Role of Child Development in Spiritual Formation

> If the sensitive period passes and your child has not made the critical discoveries, the need for that knowing remains as an inner unappeased hunger. That hunger can be what brings us as adults back to the God of our beginning years. We can watch the child's way with God and let it become part of us, helping us find our way out of the stuck and lost places far removed from the God of our childhood.[2]

Through her work with young children, Montessori determined that children from birth through approximately age two have a strong need for order and movement. This sensitive period of time is optimum for meeting those needs.

Need for Order

A baby or toddler needs an environment where things are in their own places. It helps prepare them for understanding certain aspects of time and space. Routines that respect these aspects of time and space are important. An example of this would be to choose a place where your child is changed.

Our newest grandson's parents have done this for him. My daughter always called his changing table the "happy place" because he most often responded to being placed there with a lot of baby talk, smiles, and playful movement. The baby knew what to expect in that place. It was reassuring and comforting to know what would always happen there.

This adherence to time and place need not be rigid, but rather, the norm more often than not. The same principle applies to feeding times. The place you feed becomes a familiar and comforting place. Regular, but not rigid, routines for feeding and bathing all contribute to this sense of well-being that is so important for the development of trust, the first building block of healthy emotional development. A child is more likely to become a person capable of establishing order because it has been internalized so early during the appropriate or sensitive time.

Need for Movement

Inside the womb the baby is already moving and stretching even though the space gets increasingly tighter. After birth a child needs opportunities to express movement freely. It provides them with a way to interact with the environment and the people in it. It helps them gain indepen-

---

2. Stonehouse, *Joining Children on the Spiritual Journey*, 183.

dence. That means that I can do what I need to do and I can reach the things and persons I want to be with without having to depend on others to get me there.

Understanding that need will help a parent decide how to dress a child and where to place them so that the child can move freely. It does not mean a child can go everywhere and have everything at their disposal.

Social-Emotional Development

The social-emotional development area, or doorway, is labeled *SE* on the diagram. A solid foundation of trust and autonomy, which develop in the first and second years of life, are absolutely essential if a child is ever going to be able to develop faith in a God they cannot see with their eyes or feel with their hands.

Between the ages of two to three, children know that they are separate people from their parents, but they still want and need to do things with them. Autonomy, or the need to do something oneself, is the word chosen by Erik Erikson, a developmental theorist, to describe this social-emotional stage. Children move quickly back and forth between the need for independence and dependence on others. They develop in a way that lets them know that they are separate, autonomous individuals capable of relating to others in meaningful ways. This enables them to live in a community and to live out their lives, which came from God, with others.

From four to six years old, children move into Erikson's *Initiative* stage of development. What busy little beavers they are as they flit from one area of interest to another at lightning speed. They may not finish what they start, but they are certainly capable of starting a lot of things.

Erikson's next stage, called the period of *Industry*, takes place between ages seven and twelve. This is when children learn to perfect the abilities they have acquired thus far and expand their knowledge of themselves, their world, and others in it. At this stage a child can be invited to help plan family activities, for example. They need space and time to practice their new skills and to choose their own activities.

During this time we also see the beginnings of sensitivity toward culture. Wider cultural experiences beyond home and family become important for their development. As they gain more exposure to cultures outside the familiar home environment, they will ask more and more questions about the reasons for everything. In fact, children at this age often ask up to five hundred questions a day, as compared to the average eight questions per day an adult might ask. Clear responses, a healthy dose of patience, and wisdom from God to respond to the difficult questions they ask can help children become the people God created them to be.

NEED FOR PROTECTION

Just as with infants, the early childhood and school-age children have needs that must be met during this stage of their growth and development. This is the optimum time for them to experience a loving and protective God. Cavalletti says that they have a strong need for protection. A child's need for protection goes further than that of parental protection. It is a time for being loved and protected by God, enjoying God's love and responding to Him in love. This love relationship is the firm foundation on which an obedient and trusting child can live out a moral life before God and man.

Because Christ is the fullest picture we have of God, it makes sense to center on the person of Jesus when talking about God's love for children. The Good Shepherd parable found in John 10 is a perfect example of this kind of protective love. The shepherd knows his sheep and calls them by name. How wonderfully secure a child feels knowing the Good Shepherd knows them by name. Their name is their most important source of identity. This parable also calls them outside of themselves since the Good Shepherd loves all the sheep in the fold in the same way. It meets them in all those sensitive places with the perfect picture of protective love.

The second parable is the story of the "found sheep" from Luke 15. Again the theme is protection and is experienced in the story when the shepherd goes after the lost sheep, finds it, and lovingly brings it back to the fold for safe keeping. Not only do children need the protective quality of love, but they are also at the stage where their personalities are being formed by the relationships they have. These parables meet both those basic needs.

The greatest impact on children comes from knowing they are known and loved by the Good Shepherd rather than the giving of His life for the sheep. Later, when they are in the next sensitive period, children will find meaning in the Good Shepherd's life-giving gift.[3]

---

3. Cavalletti, *Religious Potential of the Child,* 174.

A young mother of two young children wrote to me about her understanding of God's protective care:

> Every child is a lover and seeker of truth. Being made by God, we are only at home and at peace when we find our proper place nestled (like a bird in its nest) in rest and submission to His power. Likewise, children, to be happy, at peace, and secure, must find their place as one nestled in submission to their parents' discipline and at rest in their parents' love. Here too is a key for a child's emotional environment. They must know without a doubt that their parents love can never be exhausted or broken even when they disobey. Discipline must be present to bring them back into their place—the nest—which is defined by what is expected of them. With us too—all God's children—we are always totally and completely loved by God. And He calls us to remain or abide in His love. In the Old Testament, He disciplined us to bring us back under the safety of His covenant of protection and He did this because of His love for us. This is the model for us as parents.

Older school-age children do not lose their need for this kind of protective love but will respond to it and move out into new life situations knowing that they are safe and secure in God's protective care. The Good Shepherd parable unfolds for them in new ways as they come to understand and apply it in a variety of situations because its message has gone so deep.

Cognitive Development

The cognitive, or intellectual, development of a child is labeled *C* on the diagram. During the course of childhood, children move through the layers of language as diagramed by the author, Jerome Berryman—from silence to story, to codes of law, into theology, and back again. The sense of wonder that begins in the silent layer of language explained in chapter 5 is a stimulus toward cognitive growth. It is devastating to a child's development when this sense of surprise or amazement is diminished too early. One way to keep it alive is to encourage a child to play outdoors. It provides rich opportunities for experiencing amazement, wonder and awe which are responses to the language of silence. It speaks to the heart and the mind.

Your child's ability to think develops rapidly as they move from needing concrete signs or pictures in order to understand simple con-

The Role of Child Development in Spiritual Formation

cepts to being able to draw conclusions and ponder abstract concepts. They move through the layers of language, only to move back and revisit previous ones throughout the rest of their lives. Because of the importance of language for expression, Montessori, in her book *The Secret of Childhood*, has identified infancy as the optimum time for meeting this need for language.

Need for Language

It is so amazing that many babies can understand most of what you are saying to them by the time they are nine months old, even though they can't speak the language. Then the words begin to come, a few at a time, until they can converse quite easily. In order for your children to develop proficiency in speaking the language, objects and concepts must be named and repeated until they can use the language correctly and independently. Their minds are so absorbent and store more information during this time than at any other time in their lives. Language about God, about themselves, and about others will be absorbed and enrich their lives.

It can be difficult for some of you to believe that the naming of things spiritual is important in these early years. I have heard parents say that they want to wait until their child has the mental capacity to truly understand. This sounds logical, until one finds out that the heart is receptive long before the mind understands. Children know beyond their ability to understand. If the early years are bypassed or missed, it is much more difficult for an older child to simply trust; which is the basis for a faith in a God they cannot see with earthly eyes.

I mentioned earlier in the chapter that sometimes children's expressions of their understandings of God indicate they are wise beyond their years. The following story is a good example of that kind of wisdom. I remember a five-year-old boy who attended our preschool Sunday morning program. He had been part of the class during a five-week curriculum unit based upon the biblical principle that God speaks to us; that we can learn to hear His voice. Many Biblical examples were given to illustrate the principle. The little boy was puzzled by his own lack of ability to hear God's voice, and so he consequently went home and asked his mother, "How come I can't hear God's voice? What does it sound like? Why can't I hear it like Samuel?" His mother, not knowing how to respond to his questions, called me and we had a brief conversation about how she might respond to his questions.

She went back to him and talked about the things that we had discussed. Sometime after that discussion, he came running to her very excitedly and said, "Mom, mom! I just heard God's voice!" The mother asked him to tell her what he heard. The little boy replied, "It was a whisper across my heart and then it came out my head." This is a good example of a child having the ability to express with five-year-old words an experience so deep and profound and spiritual that it didn't fit within the normal range of intellectual development for his age. It was a very abstract kind of an experience to describe, and he did it well. He had an understanding that was different from and deeper than the mere acquisition of information or head knowledge. It was spiritual or mind knowledge and experience. He was able to access the language to explain it to his mother.

NEED FOR OUTSIDE PLAY

Every child needs outdoor time because there are so many opportunities for wonder and awe as they experience the beauty of nature all around them. Creation is another voice of God your children need to become accustomed to hearing, seeing, and recognizing. Without exposure to the outside environment they stand a chance of being deprived of another rich way to have relationship with God. God can so easily be introduced to them as the One who made it all.

There are children today who experience what is called "nature-deprivation." Researchers are studying this phenomenon. Creativity and imagination, plus the physical benefits of playing hard, are lost without exposure to play outside.

For many years I wondered how a child who is cognitively disabled would be able to relate to God. I came to understand that God has many doorways through which to touch all children with His love. One of the ways God does this is through a child's senses. Poet, author, and naturalist Diane Ackerman said:

> As sentient beings (having sensory capabilities) we understand and interpret the events of our lives and world by using our non-material minds. Yet the "mind," the entity of our conscious selves, is not isolated in the brain, but travels throughout the whole body on caravans of hormones and enzymes, making sense of the compounds of touch, taste, smell, hearing, and vision.
>
> By and through our human senses a sensorial impression from the midst of a religious community has been made upon the lives

The Role of Child Development in Spiritual Formation

of these children with disabilities. Becoming conscious of that qualitative world or some aspect of it depends upon a skilled and intact sensory system, which apparently is true in these cases as each individual was able to experience enough in the world in order to recompose or craft it in some understandable form. These sensory impressions have crafted and nurtured the child's ideas about where God should be worshipped and imprinted Jesus' face on the heart and mind of a child.[4]

Disabled children have imaginations that enable them to share their impressions with others in some form. For one boy, his expression was in the form of guttural sounds during worship. There was little doubt that he was participating in a very real and profound way, even though he had no capacity for language or other physical expression.

Moral Development

Moral development is labeled with an *M* in the diagram. Cavalletti believes that children under the age of six are not interested in moral behavior as such; that they are unable to receive moral formation:

> If we tried to give a child a direct moral formation we would have the same results as a nursery school teacher who wanted to tell the children about the parable of the prodigal son; the children's only reaction to this parable was the question: "what happened to those pigs?" The teacher drew the conclusion that parables are not suited to young children, whereas it was the choice of parables that was at fault. The children responded in the only way appropriate to their age: since they are in the sensitive period for protection, they were struck only by the fact that the swine were left abandoned, and the whole problem of sin and conversion completely escaped them.[5]

Morality, then, is about our whole orientation toward all of life. It comes from the depths of our being. The action side of it reveals our response to God's love, directly related to our personal experiences with Him. Because of this relationship we have a desire to act toward others with love. We are able to recognize and do what is "right" by the standards we know and respect.

As children reach the school-age years they will learn that the Good Shepherd's love is the love that forgives. They begin to see right and wrong,

---

4. Webb-Mitchell, *God Plays Piano, Too,* 113.
5. Cavalletti, *Religious Potential of the Child,* 151–52.

and justice and fairness become themes of life in all kinds of settings. This is the optimum period for the development of moral sensitivity. Cavalletti identifies their greatest need at this stage of their lives:

Need for Justice and Fairness

How many times do you hear elementary children cry out, "It isn't fair!"? Some children at this age see everything so black and white, right or wrong. Seeing the world that way makes it difficult for them to accept an opinion or belief different from their own. Conflict arises and things are said that hurt.

The need for forgiveness is present daily. What they can remember from their experience with the Good Shepherd is that the Shepherd looks for the lost sheep and when He finds it, He cleanses and binds the wounds and brings it back into the fold.

His love does not change. They need to know that God's love never fails or changes. It is as important to them as the message of the Shepherd who calls each sheep by name is to the younger child. They experience enjoyment as they relate to this story of God's unfailing love and His forgiveness.

It always amazes me to see how easily children forgive. They don't have a gunny sack full of past grievances and wounds to bring out and dump at the point a forgiveness opportunity arises. It is as if they have a special dispensation toward forgiveness. They know they are not perfect and will make mistakes as they learn to live in this world. When grace is offered to them, they learn to live gracefully with others, even when life seems unfair.

The preadolescent or young adolescent will be more likely to relate to the Good Shepherd as a role model of leadership. Children develop heroes at this stage, and the Good Shepherd is a perfect role model for them. Cavalletti identifies their need for someone to follow.

Need for a Hero Leader

Young adolescents become aware that as the Shepherd leads they are to follow. The Shepherd leads the way and they are to go where He goes. They are the followers.

The Good Shepherd certainly sets a high standard which is very appealing to this age group because they can be very enthusiastic about ideals. They have lived enough life to see that life is hard and may even feel

The Role of Child Development in Spiritual Formation

some despair or hopelessness. The Good Shepherd offers them hope and a way to live in the midst of hardship. After all, the Shepherd experiences persecution, betrayal, lies and eventually death. But He rises out of the death experience in order to offer new life to His followers. He conquers death and despair and brings real hope that there is a new way to live.

Resurrection life as the Good Shepherd lives and models it is the highest of ideals. They can aspire to it as long as they remember there are forgiveness and grace offered as they follow, stumble and fall, only to get back up and trust again that He knows the way.

This parable has so many layers that they will never be able to uncover all the richness it has to offer them as they live Kingdom life. If it is accepted and internalized, it will lead them to a rich enjoyment of God as they follow Him through whatever life sends their way. Their hearts will be formed by Him as they draw closer and closer to God in their intimate walk together. What more could a Godly parent desire than to see their child grow to be like their hero, their model, and love and enjoy Him all the days of their life?!!! It will affect all of their relationships evidenced by the love, grace, and forgiveness they offer others.

It amazes me that one story, one parable can have that kind of holding power through all child development stages. When the part of the story told matches the child's developmental need in that sensitive period of time, something miraculous happens. The truth touches the heart, where it then takes root and grows, even when the mind cannot comprehend. There is a great mystery in this!

Because God reveals Himself in everything He created, and is available anytime and anywhere, children have the opportunity to experience God in a way that lasts for a lifetime. They learn to recognize Him by sight, sound, touch, and even taste and smell. God's voice can be heard as a "whisper across my heart and then out my head," as the five-year-old mentioned earlier so aptly stated it.

DEVELOPMENT AND SPIRITUAL FORMATION

All areas of development work together to make up the whole child, as the diagram shows. For example, emotionally inspired touch, like a hug, is important to the physical well being of a child. Affirmation of a child's unique identity is important for healthy cognitive development. Children need to physically interact with their environment in order to cognitively make sense of it. Moral development depends upon social contact and information with which to base decisions about right and wrong.

We are all spiritual beings living this life in a human body. This concept is labeled *SD* on the diagram, and it covers the whole circle and everything in it. I believe that there is a spirit, or soul, in each of us that is genetically imprinted in our physical being. It was created to relate to God, spirit to spirit, for our mutual enjoyment and to fulfill His purpose for our lives.

In the Old Testament biblical account of Adam and Eve in the garden, we read about the direct mind-to-mind communication that they enjoyed with God. Their purpose for being in the garden was clear, since Got communicated directly to them after they were created. When Adam and Eve sinned, that perfect relationship was damaged and they no longer lived without shame, guilt, or fear. They could no longer see or hear God in the perfect way they had previously been able to. The act of doubting and disobeying God had destroyed their perfect communication and relationship. The capacity to relate was still there but was now covered with human imperfection.

This is where faith enters the picture. In 1 Corinthians 13:12 in the New Testament, we read, "For now we see in a mirror dimly, but then face to face; now I know in part, but then I shall know fully just as I also have been fully known." As a Christian we can be sure that things will not always be as they are now. We will one day be as spiritually aware and connected as Adam and Eve were before that fateful event changed humanity's relationship with God.

In spite of that rift, the spirit and heart of a child is not clouded by reason, intellect, and experience like an adult's is. The veil between this life and the spiritual world is much thinner. Their spiritual sense is as open and ready to be developed as it ever will be in their lives. This is the time for the development of spiritual awareness and connection. This is the time for Christ to be formed in them. This is the time to begin the lifelong process of loving and being loved by God.

A PARENT'S JOB

Hopefully, as parents we can come to know our children so well that we know their patterns of development, their needs, and their particular behaviors at home. This kind of familiarity is similar to the way we get to know God. When you follow God's lead you come to know Him intimately

The Role of Child Development in Spiritual Formation

so that you can recognize His tracks in your life. Because you know Him, you can help your children learn God's signs as well. They can rest in the knowledge that God is always there, waiting to be found and enjoyed. A deep faith develops that enables children to trust when things go wrong.

Just as a religious system provides a framework for trust and subsequent faith to develop, so do stages of child development provide the framework for spiritual formation in the heart and life of a child. A solid foundation of trust and love in the earliest years builds faith during the school-age years and leads to hope in the preadolescent and adolescent years when life can feel hopeless. The ultimate goal is for children to fall in love with Jesus, enjoy and obey Him, and deepen the relationship throughout their entire lives. They can then reach out to others and touch them with the love of God they have experienced. Best of all, you get to share in your children's joy as you grow and develop alongside them. "When we help children to encounter God we are responding to their unspoken request: 'Help me to come close to God. Help me to be fully who I am.'"[6]

QUESTIONS TO CONSIDER

1. Which area of development provides the best doorway to your child's heart?

2. Which area of development provides the best doorway to your heart?

3. What changes might this understanding bring to your relationship with your children?

4. What meaning does the phrase "a spiritual being in a human body" have for you?

5. What questions might this phrase raise for you?

---

6. Cavalletti, *The Good Shepherd & The Child*, 11.

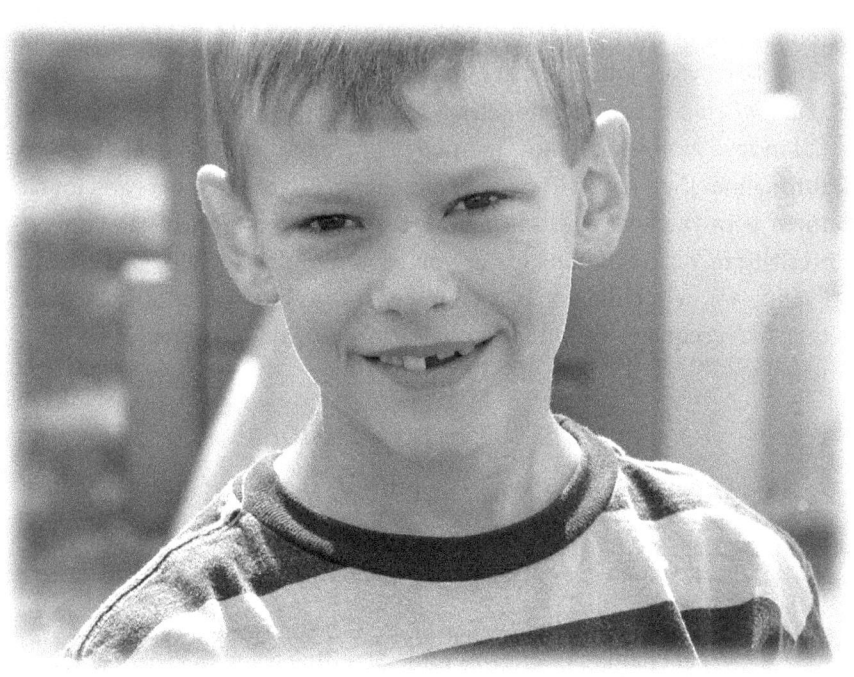

7

The Rhythm of Life and Spiritual Formation

*He has made everything appropriate in its time.
He has also set eternity in their heart.*

—Ecclesiastes 3:11

Children grow up so quickly. Every month babies go through major changes in their development. From twelve months to school age they change every six months, going from periods of equilibrium to disequilibrium. This is one of the reasons why a five-year-old who loved going to preschool suddenly does not want to go to kindergarten. The child, who was independent, has a new need for attachment once again to his mother. It is that protective love need that draws him or her back and is stronger than the child's need for autonomy and industry, as mentioned in chapter 6.

From school age through adolescence, children change yearly. These changes may cause consternation for you as the parent because the child you thought you really knew last year is suddenly standing defiantly before you, challenging you. I remember when my first daughter at age ten became, overnight, someone I didn't know. I recall asking myself, "Where did my child go?" I was not a happy mother and did not know about the necessary developmental changes that happen in a regular, rhythmic way at the appropriate times. Now I have a better understanding of those changes and the importance of them to help children move toward a healthy adult life.

How do you keep track of all of these changes and basic needs that present themselves on a daily basis, especially if you have more than one child? It all happens so quickly. There is a great urge to get it right because you realize as a parent you will never have that same chance again and the sensitive period for your child will have passed. Before you fall into despair, I want to offer hope as we look at how to establish healthy and holy rhythms in your household that facilitate this kind of attention to the growth and needs of your children—especially growth of the spirit.

THE ROLE OF RHYTHM

You might be wondering how you are ever going to fulfill the role of the sacred connector or nurturer of your child's spiritual life when we live in such a fast-paced society. Rhythm implies movement to a beat, slow or fast, steady or fluctuating, ebbing or flowing. It is not always predictable and cannot be anticipated. If you can't meet your children's needs because the pace gets too fast, hurried, or full, you might have to step out of sync with the rhythms you have become accustomed to until you can find a more natural, comfortable one for your family.

Most of us would agree that it feels more comfortable to be in sync rather than out of sync, particularly with your family members. While uncomfortable for a time, however, it is more beneficial to be out of sync if being in sync has outcomes or consequences that don't match your life goals personally or professionally. For example, productivity, efficiency, and effectiveness are highly prized commodities in the working world. Getting to the bottom of a pile, checking off tasks that are completed, and getting everywhere you were supposed to be in the amount of time allotted to you for the day are supposed to make you feel like you've accomplished something of value. As soon as that is felt and acknowledged, you must start again in the same way the next day in order to accomplish it again. And on and on it goes; the push and the pressure are never-ending.

Is that the way we are to live in order to live an abundant kingdom life? What happens to children who find their lives governed by the same forces when everything in them says, "but I want to play or stay home?" How can we pay attention to the voice of God in us and around us when our minds are racing three miles ahead of where our bodies are? How can we learn a different way of living from the children in our care if all of life seems like a race to be won? How can we live a mindful life in the midst of the chaotic milieu all around us?

We all fall prey to the mechanism called "entrainment," which is the process by which life rhythms fall into synchronization with each other. It can be a "stuck" place. When we are in that synchronized place, often we do not consciously realize we need to change it. Even when we do recognize something is wrong, we don't know how to change it. We lose the ability to shift time; to know how to pause, reflect, contemplate, and think in order to go from the frenetic to the peaceful, to truly relax, to take note, or even to feel. We have forgotten how to rest. Dr. Stephen Rechtshaffen in his book *Timeshifting: Creating More Time to Enjoy Life* says:

> We must entrain with rhythms other than societies. And we are best off, I think, starting with our own. One of the simplest and most effective ways to become present in our life is to pay attention to our breathing. Breathing is a way of bringing us mentally and emotionally back to center; it is a deep and integrating rhythm of the body. By allowing ourselves to be come conscious of our breathing, we begin to slow down into the breath and allow ourselves to set a rhythm for the body that is peaceful, calm, and healthy.
>
> Try it now! Fill your lungs completely, slowly, and let the air out slowly, deliberately. Do it a few times. "Feel" your breath as it comes in, feel it as it goes out. . . . Closing your eyes is particularly helpful. Our eyes scan the world, mirroring the flitting and skimming of our mind, and shutting them draws us out of the automatic, almost robotic rhythm to which we entrain without realizing it. Rhythm is powerful, sometimes you must fight against it, sometimes let yourself go with it. Knowing whether to fight it or flow with it depends, first, on recognizing it for what it is. Begin by simply becoming aware of different rhythms as you go through your days. Do that and you can learn to change them, and by so doing, set your own pace.[1]

GOD'S VOICE IN SCRIPTURE

In Ecclesiastes 3:1–8 we read about God's established order for the rhythms of life: "There is an appointed time for everything. And there is a time for every event under heaven." Time as we know it belongs to this world.

> A time to give birth, and a time to die;
> A time to plant, and a time to uproot what is planted.
> A time to kill, and a time to heal;
> A time to tear down, and a time to build up.
> A time to weep, and a time to laugh;
> A time to mourn, and a time to dance.
> A time to throw stones, and a time to gather stones;

---

1. Rechtshaffen, *Timeshifting: Creating More Time to Enjoy Life,* 78.

A time to embrace, and a time to shun embracing.
A time to search, and a time to give up as lost;
A time to keep, and a time to throw away.
A time to tear apart, and a time to sew together;
A time to be silent, and a time to speak.
A time to love, and a time to hate;
A time for war, and a time for peace.

There are other natural rhythms that provide a sense of order in our world that were established from the beginning. As recorded in the creation stories from the book of Genesis, God established a rhythm for work and rest. Six days for work and one day for rest was the order God sanctioned and set as an example for the first human inhabitants of the earth. That rhythm was practiced by Jewish people for centuries and is still followed by many today. The practice of resting on the seventh day is healthy and allows time and space for the Holy.

I clearly remember the rhythm my parents set in our household when I was growing up. Every Saturday my mother cleaned and cooked in preparation for Sunday. The floors were scrubbed and polished to a high sheen. The house was filled with aromas of good food. I got my bath and was put to bed at the end of the day, full of anticipation for the day to come. From my viewpoint, everything was ready and all was right with the world. Our house was clean. My clothes were pressed and waiting to be worn during the next day. All I had to do was sleep well and wake up refreshed, ready for church and the relaxed pace of the rest of the day. To my young mind these were such simple pleasures. I still get those same feelings of total contentment after I have completed my work on Saturday and relax in the knowledge that I am ready for a change of pace and rest the next day.

In the New Testament, Jesus refers to the need for rest when He reminds His followers that they could come to Him for rest when they were weary of spirit and burdened by life's weights. Jesus said to His followers in Matthew 11:28–30, "Come to Me, all who are weary and heavy-laden, and I will give you rest. Take My yoke upon you, and learn from Me, for I am gentle and humble in heart; and you shall find rest for your souls. For My yoke is easy, and My load is light."

As parents, we can show our children how to live life with periods of restful activity or inactivity between the times of hard work and stressful responsibilities. They will learn to live this way themselves if it is modeled in their home growing up. Time and space can be ordered and set aside for rejuvenation. Everyone in the family will benefit from it. They do not have to grow up living on the same fast track we find ourselves on so often. We can show them another way to live.

OTHER VOICES

Changing our own pace and response to life's challenges and pressures will affect us, as adults, in our transformation process. Consequently, it will affect how we parent our children of all ages. In their young years, children have no choice but to live the rhythm of life set by their parents. We control their environment and, subsequently, the pace at which they move and live. Rhythm is the force upon which every activity of the day moves. It can have a profound impact on what children remember and how they ultimately choose to live.

Something as common and ordinary as preparing a meal can have an impact on how one remembers and lives out their life. I heard a story about a village in Malawi where the rhythms of life are passed on from one generation to the next. It involves the process of preparing the maize for their daily meal. The women would stand while pounding grain in a mortar. The mortar and pestle were very large, almost as tall as the shortest woman. The children would sit around and watch the women prepare the maize. When this was done, the women would mix it with boiling water and stir it briskly while it thickened. Later that day, the porridge they had made would be served to the whole family.

The noise they made while pounding the maize with the pestles in the mortars was rhythmic, and the women hummed along with it. As they would become aware of the sounds they were making, the women would change the speed and pattern of their pounding. Another woman would begin to sing instead of hum. Eventually, the random sound of preparing the maize would turn into a musical event.

One of the young boys, who was watching, noticed how the percussive noise and the sounds of the women's voices blended into a beautiful traditional song. Thirty years later he is playing in a band called Wenge Musica. As he listens to his music played back, he thinks of his mother and aunts back in the village singing their songs while they pound the maize during the normal routines of their daily life.

Those who garden as part of their daily lives experience seasonal rhythms. They wait for the bulbs to flower; the vegetables to mature; and the trees to grow, blossom, and produce fruit. There is such satisfaction that comes from having tended the soil, pulled the weeds, and harvested the crops. It is hard work but well worth it.

Gardeners experience delayed gratification and so do their families who go through the whole process of food production before they get to eat any of it. There are no hamburgers in a matter of seconds. We are so used to instant gratification in this culture.

People of different cultures live in a rhythm different from our own. When Jesus walked this earth, He showed us a worthy example of balance and structure in a very busy life. He lived as we are to live. By all human standards, Jesus certainly was a busy man. In fact, He was so busy that the disciples were afraid He would go mad because He was so seldom left alone. People followed Jesus wherever He went, necessitating private withdrawals for the refreshment of His spirit and connection with His Father. He had to give God His undivided attention and His body a chance to relax and rest. During these moments Jesus experienced an "awareness of His identity, His mission, and His relationship with God. He could see God's kingdom in its entirety.

We need to do the same, but it is not easy. Author and former Yale professor Henri Nouwen, said:

> It is hard to leave our people, our job, and the hectic places where we are needed, in order to be with the One from whom all good things come. Yet, once we flop in the chair, we realize we need such a time, such a place for God. And such a time as this can unmask the illusion of busyness, usefulness, and indispensability. It is a way of being empty and useless in the presence of God and of proclaiming our basic belief that all is grace and nothing is simply the result of hard work."[2]
>
> The world doesn't need more busy people, maybe not even more intelligent people. It needs "deep people," people who know that they need solitude if they are going to find out who they are;[3]

In order for our children to become "deep people," they too need order, healthy rhythms, space, and solitude to sit with the questions that

---

2. Nouwen, *The Living Reminder: Service and Prayer in Memory of Jesus Christ*, 51–52.

3. Postema, *Space for God*, 16.

The Rhythm of Life and Spiritual Formation

all human beings need to ask themselves: "Who am I, who made me, why am I here, and what am I doing in all this activity and noise?" When you are in a place of "being" rather than "doing," you have time and the presence of mind to listen for the quiet inner voice that speaks in words not understood by the mind but by the heart and spirit. These are questions worth pondering.

CHILDREN'S RHYTHMS OF SILENCE AND ACTIVITY

Remember the five-year-old who said God's voice was a "whisper across my heart and out my head"? Children do not have to be all grown up to expound wisdom and truth to us. We would do well to listen, watch, and learn. Scripture tells us in Isaiah 11:6 "that a child shall lead them." Children know the language of silence because they have most recently experienced it. We need to leave our theology behind and once again cycle back to reenter that world of wonder full of *aahs, ahas,* and *ha-has.* And what better way to recapture our childlikeness than to journey back alongside our children.

In her book *Something More,* Jean Grasso Fitzpatrick writes about silence and the child and invites parents to reexamine their own thinking about it:

> Silence is not something we tend to associate with our children. The moment we begin to suspect they are "too quiet," don't we rush off to find out what mischief they're up to?
>
> We may even assume that silence is a waste of time for children, who have so much to learn. "If we're waiting in the doctor's office or in line somewhere, I try to get my daughter thinking, rather than just sitting there letting our minds do nothing," one mother of a five-year-old girl told me. "So I drill her any time we have the chance—letters, numbers, and parts of the body."
>
> Far from being a waste of time, the quiet, unproductive moments in our children's lives can be profoundly meaningful and sustaining. Silence should not be forced on a child. Yet it can be presented as an opportunity for us to set aside the day's cares so that we can be attentive to and aware of the deeper truths that speak within our hearts, to "listen at the stillness."[4]

In his *Memoirs of a Quaker Boyhood,* Rufus Jones recalls his own early appreciation of silence during Quaker meetings. He was a little boy

---

4. Fitzpatrick, *Something More: Nurturing Your Child's Spiritual Growth,* 146.

full of animal energy who, you would think, would have a hard time sitting on a hard bench with his legs dangling while being absolutely quiet. In fact, at times, he would find himself wishing he could hit the boy in front of him over the head instead of sitting in silence. But, only for a moment. That kind of play would have to wait. He describes the silence as a kind of spell that would come over him. It was so palpable that even as a young boy he could feel it. You might say he had a sense of the divine presence.

Jones goes on to say in his memoir that he was never given an explanation of the doctrine of silence. He just simply experienced it. Jones says that the practice of silence was something that stayed with him in his adult life. Sitting still in a motionless group while concentrating on God's divine presence had a profound impact on his life, something he still treasures.

Two of my favorite educators have thoughts about children's experience of silence as well. Maria Montessori, an Italian educator, observed that children are very aware of the richness and fullness of silence. When she worked with children in the slums of Rome, she would introduce them to what she called the "silence lesson." As soon as she would begin to write the word "silence" on the blackboard, the whole class would stop working and become perfectly still. These children were only three, but they enjoyed silence. Montessori believed this was true because they experienced it at a time when they needed protective love and care, which the silence provided. They could be in touch with God, who was their loving protector.

Fitzpatrick agrees with Montessori when she says that, even without instruction, the youngest children can experience the presence of God in the absence of noise. She writes about an experience she had when speaking to a group of first-graders. She told them that when she was young, she had expected God's loud voice would come from underneath the altar. One girl, with an indignant tone, told her that it doesn't because God talks to us in our hearts, not from under the altar. Children can speak with such conviction about what they believe to be truth.

A friend and colleague with two young children made "God boxes" for her children that contained symbols and reminders of God's presence in their lives. They were tangible items that held some meaning for them, because they had been allowed to touch them and know the significance of each item in the box. During naptime, each child could choose to sleep or to play with the items in their God box. If they chose not to sleep, naptime remained a quiet time in which they could explore the richness that each item brought to them in their interaction with it. This practice was a very meaningful time for the children, providing something tangible to help them experience God as they remembered and related to each item. Setting aside time and space to do the same kind of remembering and relating could benefit all of us.

OUR RESPONSIBILITY

We need to give our children time and space to grow and learn the ways of God. It is an important job and can easily overwhelm us. We need to be careful not to lose sight of the real goal, which is freedom to live completely and fully in the present moment where God resides with us. After all, God sent His only Son to give us life so that we might live abundantly. I don't believe an abundant life can be measured in the same way we check our progress on task lists and appointments. We will come to know the freedom of a child as we leisurely move through the moments, knowing the value because we are walking those moments with God.

John Piper, a pastor who wrote *Leisure, The Basis of Culture,* says:

> Leisure is a receptive attitude of mind, a contemplative attitude, and it is not only the occasion but also the capacity for steeping oneself in the whole of creation.
>
> Leisure is not the attitude of mind of those who actively intervene, but of those who are open to everything; not of those who grab and grab hold, but of those who leave the reins loose and who are free and easy themselves—almost like someone falling asleep, for one can only fall asleep by "letting oneself go." . . . When we really let our minds rest contemplatively on a rose in bud, on a child at play, on a divine mystery, we are rested and quickened as though by a dreamless sleep. . . . It is in these silent receptive moments that the soul of man is sometimes visited by an awareness of what holds the world together.[5]

A life lived with God then will have an ebb and flow between spending and refreshing it and rest and relationship with Him. It will resemble that of a child's approach to the moments of the day. After all, it is most often young children who cannot wait to get up and get started on their day. They face the day with exuberance, spend their moments in concen-

---

5. Piper, *Leisure, The Basis of Culture,* 40–42.

trated and focused activity, and soak up what there is to learn and experience in their play and interactions with others. They cry when wounded by another but forgive so quickly and easily. They know where to go to get help and are not ashamed to ask for it. They do not gunnysack their woes but give up their wound in order to experience the joy of playing once again. Gratitude pours from their beings as they engage so completely in the wonder of the present moment. Although they truly know the meaning of real leisure and can live without having to preplan and execute every waking moment, I believe they still need structure and order.

RHYTHM FOR INFANTS, TODDLERS, AND PRESCHOOLERS

As was stated in chapter 6, infants, toddlers, and preschoolers experience a need for order that provides a structured rhythm for them. They get hungry and get fed. They get sleepy and they rest. They need comfort and get held and comforted. They need to be refreshed and they get bathed. There is an ebb and flow to their day based on nothing other than meeting their specific needs of the moment. Even their optimum times for learning have a rhythm to them. They need order, movement, and language. A parent moves in and out of these, weaving them into the tapestry of daily life as they care for the child, supplying the essential building blocks of life. The entire household has to move in these rhythms in order for the young child's needs to be met. The rhythms are different than those experienced by the parent in their working world, and thus parents often feel out of sync. They get tired, trying to learn new rhythms that seem to leave no room for the fast, striving pace of today's society.

The arrival of our first-born introduced a new way of living to me. I was at home with my daughter during the day while my husband worked. During the evening, he cared for her. In the first months, I slept when she slept and ate after she ate. I would try to stay on top of the laundry pile one load at a time. She ate every hour and a half because she was a preemie, so the rhythm of the day did not include a lot in my personal agenda.

But I grew to love the new rhythm. The time we spent together was creating an incredible bond. I found I could read during those nighttime feedings and find my own soul refreshed. The rhythm was comfortable—like riding smooth waves in the ocean. What didn't get done in a day could wait until the next. The natural order of daytime and nighttime didn't exist in the same way. It all flowed together with small periods of rest and withdrawal to revitalize.

It was quite a different scenario with the addition of each subsequent child. With a toddler or two in addition to a new baby, our daily rhythms had to be adjusted to include everyone. As I reflect on that now, I do not remember it as a difficult time. It certainly was all consuming, but I knew it was important to give the time that was needed for each child's growth and development. They needed order in their day and in their environment. There were places to be fed, changed, and played with; consistent times for the necessary routines of the day because they were important. They needed to move freely in a safe environment and experiment in order to learn the skills necessary for doing things themselves. They needed to develop their language capacity, and that required face-to-face conversation and my complete attention.

Again, our family rhythm changed when my children reached the late preschool and early elementary years. There was more time I could call my own. Schedules allowed for larger blocks of time to be devoted to the things that needed to be done and the things we chose to do. The new rhythms felt so freeing. It wasn't until we began to schedule the kids' after-school activities that we felt the change in rhythms again. We had to adjust in each season as their involvement in activities outside the home changed. It became increasingly more difficult to manage it all when I began to go back to work full-time. My situation was not unusual or unique. It is what many parents find themselves facing today. The rhythm of life is manageable, but the fluctuations affect every aspect of their lives together.

RHYTHM FOR ELEMENTARY KIDS

While attending my grandson's football game, I overheard a conversation by a group of mothers who were overwhelmed with the number of things they had to squeeze into their day. They talked about dropping off one child at basketball practice while on their way to drop off another at football practice. Some of them had their boys in hockey as well. And, of course, there were girls in some of the families who had gymnastics and dance or music lessons. It made me dizzy listening to them talk. One mother, in particular, talked so fast that it was difficult to understand her. She sounded like she was running on adrenaline all the time in order to keep up with her family's schedule. I remember thinking as I eavesdropped, "When do the kids get to play and initiate their own free time activity? Do they have free time?"

A week later, I happened to meet an elementary band instructor at the theater. In the course of our conversation, he told me he has never had such a low retention rate in all of his years of teaching. He told me he had started thirty-six students in the fall on their band instruments and had only ten left by the end of the year. The kids had no time for practice. We talked about some of the other possible reasons for low numbers of returning students. Parents have to help kids develop a regular habit of practice by establishing a time and place for it to happen. If the practice schedule is haphazard, the child will not develop the skills necessary for the enjoyment of the instrument or the music. Establishing a regular routine and monitoring it is essential for success and the development of personal discipline.

For programs outside the home, parents are responsible to get their children there, pay the bill, and pick them up for the trip home. Many parents do not get to establish routines and schedules for skill building in those programs because the coaches do it. I heard my grandson's football coach deciding when the tournament was going to be held based on when he and his son were available. They were both involved in hockey and had to work football around it. Everyone is doing a balancing act with many spinning plates. It is a fact of life in many of America's families today.

I believe over programming children is a common problem for many families today. New rhythms have to be established in order to make the schedule work. For example, my grandsons get started on their homework right after school and then get some time of their own. I am so grateful that their parents have not over programmed them with back-to-back scheduled activities each day. They need time to develop relationships with friends and spend time with other family members. Kids also need time to settle down. After an evening event they need to slow down the mind and body in order to sleep well and wake up refreshed for a new day. Otherwise, their bodies will adapt to the high adrenaline level and get stuck there for the rest of their lives.

By examining how you are living in this culture, you can make choices for your children that reflect your values and new understandings. It is not easy to do that in our society, but it is possible. The dividends will be huge, and you will not regret it.

The Rhythm of Life and Spiritual Formation

QUESTIONS TO CONSIDER

1. What changes need to be made in your life?
2. As your children's nurturer, what changes do you need to make for them?
3. As your children's blesser, what needs to be different in their lives?
4. In which of these roles do you feel most confident as it relates to establishing healthy rhythms of life for your children?
5. Are you experiencing the blessing from living in sync with His rhythms?

8

The Role of Ritual, Symbol, and Celebration in Spiritual Formation

> *When your children ask you, 'what are these stones to you?' you'll say, 'The flow of the Jordan was stopped in front of the Chest of the Covenant of God as it crossed the Jordan—stopped in its tracks. These stones are a permanent memorial for the People of Israel.'*
>
> —Joshua 4:6b–7[1]

Rituals and symbols foster a sense of continuity, identity, and stability, which are important for spiritual formation. They are valuable for more than just intentional ceremonies, however. They serve the same purpose in everyday life and everyday activities.

RITUALS IN THE HOME

Some of the structured rhythms of the day contain rituals that give meaning and purpose to an activity. Marjorie Thompson, a Presbyterian minister, defines ritual as "an intentional ceremony, a repeatable rite that uses symbolic acts with or without words to express and carry the meaning of our faith."[2] Symbols, rituals, and structures are a means of growth. Every family needs to decide which ones serve a valuable purpose for their family and then establish them as a regular part of their life together.

Everyday rituals act a little like punctuation marks on the rhythms of the day. It has been interesting to watch my eight-month-old grandson respond to the rituals that are a part of his day. He knows that when he is placed on the changing table, it is time for some serious vocalizing and

---

1. Mason, *The Message,* 366–67.
2. Thompson, *FAMILY The Forming Center,* 91.

chatter. He hears "You are My Sunshine," a song that has been sung to him since before he was born, and he tries to join in. All of this is familiar, comforting, and what he anticipates every time his diaper is changed. There are other rituals that punctuate his day, such as his mother planting kisses all over his face before she puts him down to sleep. Her kisses have a calming affect on him and he goes to sleep easily after this ritual is performed.

Others have told me about the rituals they established with their children. One mother hung a small cross beside her baby's crib. Every night before she puts him to bed, she tells him why he was named Jeremiah and recites some words from scripture to him about his identity. Then she prays a blessing over him and finishes by tracing the shape of the cross on the wall with her finger. She makes the sign of the cross on his forehead and closes with the words, "In the name of the Father, Son, and Holy Spirit." Her baby seems to look forward to that time and now blesses her by making the sign of the cross on her forehead before he goes to bed.

Such rituals do not guarantee a spiritual experience. They are merely tools to help us convey something—whether that's marking a certain moment of the day, signaling a change in activities, or expressing something about our spirituality. Rituals may also signify a celebration, whether in the home or the faith community. Gertrud Mueller Nelson, a Montessori teacher and author, says, "The core of a celebration speaks to the hearts of all humankind—in all times and in all places. It speaks the symbolic language of the soul and is hardly ever practical, but more poetic, playful, prayerful. . . . Ceremony makes the ordinary extraordinary."[3]

RITUALS IN THE COMMUNITY

When I think about common rituals in the community, I am reminded of the rituals I witnessed in my sister's home in Jerusalem. Saturday night was the time when Jewish Christians gathered for the close of Shabbat. They began their home meeting with several rituals. First, two boys carried in a large scroll and took its cover off while the rabbi held the scroll. After a reading of the portion of scripture chosen for that night, a three-stranded candle was lit. Wine was poured full to overflowing. Songs were sung by the adults and children gathered there. A prayer shawl was then held up over the heads of all the children while the parents prayed a blessing over

3. Nelson, *To Dance with God; Family Ritual and Community Celebration*, 150.

them. At the close of the teaching time, the candle was extinguished in the wine and a special scent box was passed around from person to person until all had a chance to smell the sweet scent. A blessing was proclaimed, and everyone prepared for the feast to follow.

Every week, the same rituals were performed. They were expected and anticipated. These same rituals meant the same thing to everyone who regularly attended the weekly meetings. The children came to know and understand the significance of each thing they did, and they were included in everything from the time they were very young. The rituals punctuated the meeting so everyone knew what followed next. They involved objects that symbolized a spiritual truth that was spoken about every time they were together. My favorite part of the whole evening was the smelling of the spices in the special silver box, which was done to help us to carry the remembrance of the resurrection of Jesus into the new week. The presence of Jesus in their lives was to be remembered as a sweet fragrance that accompanied them wherever they went.

SYMBOLS IN RITUALS

Symbols are often an important part of rituals. For example, the lighting of a candle during the celebration of the birth of Jesus symbolizes the coming of the light of God into the world. The sharing of the bread and the cup at a communion service brings to mind an event called Passover and Christ's words to His disciples as He broke the bread and drank the wine with them at the Last Supper before His death.

A symbol works in several ways: it is something in and of itself, but it also suggests something more. A symbol is different from a metaphor, which makes a comparison between two dissimilar things. An example of a metaphor is "His life was a candle that had just been snuffed out." Symbols associate with things, but their meanings are both literal and figurative. A symbol might be the candle itself, which would bring to mind the reflected light of Christ.

Some symbols, such as a cross worn around a person's neck, have commonly accepted meanings. As common as this symbol is, however, all symbols are determined by the individual and his or her community. No symbols have absolute meanings, and by their nature we cannot read symbols at face value. It is important to question the meanings of symbols, beginning by asking what they could have meant in the past.

As children begin to encounter symbols of faith, they enter into the mystery and wonder of what faith might mean and will gradually come to know in fuller ways what the group they belong to believes it means. Sofia Cavalletti says, "The person who beholds a sign or a symbol realizes that whatever level of understanding has been attained there is another level and yet another, and so it continues without ever reaching its depth. The person who contemplates the sign sees reality with a sense of wonder that is always growing. . . . Wonder is the offspring of the contemplative spirit in us."[4]

Some symbols will be used in the home; others in the larger faith community. In the faith community, light, bread, juice or wine, and water are some of the basic signs or symbols. The parables of Jesus are symbolic stories that can relate to the experiences people face today. To help children understand these stories, give them time to pause and think about their symbolic meanings. They are very capable of doing this—to think about and consider the meaning of the symbol, but it is important to read parables slowly so that the meaning can be discerned. By helping them focus, they can stop and be still. If they are interrupted too quickly or too often, they are likely to resist learning, which can result in a show of indifference.

NEW MEANINGS FOR OLD CELEBRATIONS

As a child, I remember how I looked forward to celebrating Halloween in our rural, small-town community. It truly was my favorite holiday celebration. We had the run of the whole town as we collected treat after treat in our large pillowcases. People made delicious things to give to us and we felt welcome when we arrived at their door. Hours later, it was so much fun to dump out the bag and look at what had been given to us. I don't remember eating it all, but I remember the fun of going with my friends on this great adventure.

While this was not a religious or spiritual holiday celebration, I came away from it with a sense of the divine. It was such a beautiful time of year. I loved the way the warm fall colors wrapped me up in their beauty. The leaves crunching underneath my feet released their wet fragrance, and I wanted to be totally immersed in the wonder of them. I loved the season for its magnificent color and intoxicating smells. It also spoke of a time yet

---

4. Cavalletti, Coulter, *The Good Shepherd & The Child*, 38.

to come and the time that had passed. All time stood still as we celebrated that moment, that one night a year that was so rich and full. Halloween was a memory maker that drew me closer to God as the Creator. I loved the world He had placed me in. It was beautiful and safe.

Christmas was another favorite holiday. My favorite decorations were the special lights on the Christmas tree that bubbled when they got hot. I would turn out the lights in our living room and lay on my stomach looking at the Christmas tree for long periods of time. I noticed the few presents under the tree but was mostly interested in the smell of the tree and the beautiful lights that made everything look magical.

We had a regular ritual on Christmas Eve. My sisters and I always got dressed in the new outfits that came as gifts from my grandmother in California. Then we headed off to the two churches where my father pastored for their Christmas Eve services. My favorite service took place in the little country town of Mannanah with its total of fifty residents. The children always put on a Christmas program, and the singing of the Christmas music was my favorite part. How I loved to hear those carols!

When it was all over, we headed home to eat our Christmas Eve meal. The meal was a fancy one, which meant there were many dishes to be washed when we were finished eating. We could not open gifts until the dishes were done. Then we would all gather in the living room for a small program my sisters and I would put on for the adopted grandparents of my youngest sister. It seemed to take forever. We finally finished and got to open our gifts. They were few in number but brought great joy.

One particular Christmas Eve stood out from all the others because our usual rituals were not possible. The wind was howling and snow was wildly blowing. The electricity went out, which meant we had no stove for cooking dinner. My mother and father lit candles and opened a can of cold pork and beans for us to eat. We even got to eat by candlelight in front of the tree. Because we ate on paper plates, there were no dishes to wash. We had no guests, which meant we could open our gifts much sooner. I am sure our father prayed the blessing and then we took turns opening our gifts, enjoying each other as much as our gifts that night. I went to bed a very happy child. In my mind, that was the best Christmas we had ever had! Our grateful hearts brought us to a state of worship.

Parenting by Developmental Design

WORSHIP AS FAMILY CELEBRATION

Marjorie Thompson, the author of *FAMILY The Forming Center,* says that the more we become aware of the presence of God, the more we can live our lives as a celebration of His divine presence. Becoming conscious of God's spirit in the ordinary routines of our day and learning to respond takes time and practice. That is the significance of particular disciplines like family worship, seasonal rituals, and special celebrations. Both the Sabbath and genuine recreation are a means of becoming attuned to the divine presence in life and learning to respond with reverence and joy.

Wouldn't it be wonderful to experience worship that leads to celebrations in everyday life? After all, God is present in everything and everyone and He wants us to celebrate and enjoy Him. Our relationship with God cannot be based on seasonal celebrations at the appropriate time of the year. God wants us to celebrate Him and with Him every day. As we do that, we give our children a heritage built on real encounters with a Living God. They will know how to find God in the moments of the day. But we must lead the way by setting aside time and space for it to happen. Family worship can be as individual as the people participating in it. There isn't just one right way to do it.

The use of concrete symbols as part of the celebration of Christ's presence in the home is important for a child's spiritual formation. Set aside a place in your home to be used as "sacred space" for worship. Add a few simple symbols of faith that have some meaning for your children. Thompson has written the following about a possible way to do this:

> Some families have a little table set like an altar with a Bible, a candle, and perhaps a beautiful icon or homemade cross. It can be a place for spontaneous offerings: wildflowers, autumn leaves, a speckled egg, a bright feather, or other treasures collected while exploring. Parents might encourage children to collect symbols from some parables: a mustard seed from the spice rack (Matt. 13:31–32), an interesting coin (Luke 15:8–10), an artificial pearl or a white marble for the "pearl of great price" (Matt. 13:45–46). These would have their special place on or near the altar and could be used in family worship and scriptural reflection. Families might cut out figures or create clay figurines to depict shepherd and sheep or a Christmas crèche. Cavalletti reports that children love to play with such figures and can spend remarkable periods of time contemplating biblical stories with the aid of concrete ob-

The Role of Ritual, Symbol, and Celebration in Spiritual Formation

> jects. Over time, and through play, they will gradually assimilate biblical meanings.
>
> The child's need for concrete objects and physical activity in learning is part of why ritual in family worship is so essential. Rituals are embodied ways of celebrating God's presence in the midst of ordinary life. They take the common stuff of life and reveal its sacramental capacity. Always include some ritual expression in family worship rather than remain in the realm of abstract words. Adults, like children, respond inwardly to the power of symbols and actions in worship.[5]

I have seen such sacred spaces in several of my friends' homes. They are right there in the midst of their everyday living space. Anyone entering their home might see it and wonder about its use. The family's special symbols are there along with a Bible, sometimes a CD player, and even prayer shawls. Candles, ready to be lit, and a comfortable place to sit invite one to "be still and know that I am God"(Psalm 46:10). There is a very special presence in those places. When children see their parents use that space in the moments of everyday life, they will likely be drawn to try it themselves.

Prayer can become a meaningful ritual that helps connect each family member together during the course of their day. One family Thompson writes about has practiced a Morning Prayer ritual that has held its appeal for many years. She describes their breakfast meal as a time each family member shares what they expect to do during the day. They talk about what they look forward to and what they would like to avoid. Each family member receives a prayer. Because of this practice, they all feel heard, supported, and lovingly cared for as they leave for their day's activities. During the day they remember the needs of the others and pray for them. When they gather at the dinner table they have an opportunity to share the events of the day with their family. They are eager to find out how things have gone.

There are so many ways families can incorporate meaningful prayer into their daily lives. A mother I know drives her daughter to school each morning. When she stops the car to drop off her daughter, she prays a blessing over her. Her daughter expressed how much she misses it when her mom isn't able to drop her off in the morning. Other parents have taught their children "breath prayers" they can say throughout their day.

---

5. Thompson, *FAMILY The Forming Center*, 88.

These are short prayers that often come from scripture and have significance and meaning to them. Some examples might be:

- "I love you, Jesus."
- "God, have mercy on me today."
- "Thank you for my family."
- "Jesus, you are all I need."

The meaning behind these words is important so that the prayer does not become a dead ritual. After all, it is what the heart is praying that matters, not the words by themselves.

Some rituals are for private use in family celebrations, while others are conducive to sharing with others. I love the rituals established in my sister's home in Jerusalem. They often invite others to share the Shabbat meal with them on Friday night. Then they celebrate the Sabbath together the next day, culminating in their whole community's celebration on Saturday evening, which prepares them for the week to come. Shabbat comes to an end and they are ready to take the sweet memory of their time together into the new week.

In addition to their weekly gatherings, their community celebrates all the Jewish festivals together. In each of the festivals they are remembering and living out the reality of God's intervention on their behalf. The stories are told and retold, passed on from one generation to the next. I will never forget the Purim celebration that I was privileged to experience with them. Everyone came dressed in a costume and brought a noisemaker, which was used whenever Haman's name was read from the book of Esther. The entire book was read out loud while everyone sat and listened for the right moments to cheer for Esther or make noise for Haman. When it was finished, they all celebrated the deliverance of the Jewish people from their oppressors by feasting. It was indeed a spiritual celebration.

RITES OF PASSAGE AS CELEBRATIONS

There are unique rites of passage that can be celebrated within the family. Symbols are often used in these rites of passage and can be used during an annual celebration of that rite of passage. Baby baptisms or dedications are examples of this kind of rite of passage ceremony that often

The Role of Ritual, Symbol, and Celebration in Spiritual Formation

use symbols, such as water or the light of a candle. Why not celebrate the dedication or baptism each year just as we do for birthdays? After all, children learn what is important to us by what we choose to celebrate. As children get older, a parent could ask them to name the person who has been most important in their faith life this year. You could invite the named person to the celebration of your child's dedication or baptism. The person invited will be blessed to be part of it. The candle could be lit again at each subsequent celebration of the baptism or dedication. There is no right or wrong way to use the symbols. Use whatever has meaning for your family.

Celebrations that mark a child's passage into the teen years are being practiced by more families now than in the past. Many families have Bar/Bat Mitzvahs or Confirmation celebrations for their children. My twin nephews had their Bar Mitzvahs at the Western Wall in Jerusalem. They studied with an elderly rabbi for many months in preparation for this occasion. It involved the memorization and discussion of much scripture. Then they were to speak of their faith in their own words to the people who came to support them in their celebration. It was a very festive occasion and one that will be remembered for a long time.

For families that are not Jewish or don't belong to a liturgical church, other options for celebration are practiced. I have known several parents who have planned "blessing parties" for their child. The young teenager invites significant adults and peers who have had a spiritual impact on them. Each invitee prepares a special word to deliver in the form of a blessing while attaching it to a symbol that will help the message connect to the adolescent's heart as well as his or her mind. I recently attended one such party for a young girl just turning twelve. We had a tea party with all the trimmings and blessed her with significant words about the character we saw developing in her. She received gifts symbolizing these characteristics in her. One of her gifts was a special box to hold the written words and symbols that had been given to her. In years to come, these gifts will enable her to relive the experience and hopefully realize its significance.

The beauty of all of this is that there are no hard and fast rules about how to use symbol, ritual, and celebration. Your own relationship and your child's relationship with God will help you decide on those practices and celebrations that have special meaning for your family and community. Whatever you decide to do, do it regularly. Establish a healthy, consistent rhythm of life for your family. You get to establish the routines and practices that will allow for space and time to recognize and celebrate God's activity in your lives. The symbols that you choose and the rituals you practice will help make the mysteries of God something you can wonder about together. Out of your pondering together will come the formative experiences that can help shape your young image-bearers into the likeness of the God they have grown to love.

QUESTIONS TO CONSIDER

1. What rituals can you identify that have meaning for the spiritual formation of your family members?
2. Name some of the symbols and signs that are part of your rituals.
3. If you find yourself resisting the adoption of rituals, ask God to reveal to you the source of your resistance. Journal your thoughts or have a conversation with God about it.
4. What celebrations do you find meaningful for your family?
5. What celebrations would you like to introduce to your family?
6. What is God forming in your heart around celebrations?
7. What role do the celebrations you have with your family play in the spiritual formation of your children?

9

The Role of Imagination in Spiritual Formation

Jesus said, "Let the children alone, and do not hinder them from coming to Me; for the kingdom of heaven belongs to such as these."
—MATTHEW 19:14

THE GIFT OF IMAGINATION is precious and unique to our children from the moment they are born. They know how to live in the world of imagination, which has a sense of the infinite. God can lift their hearts to undreamed possibilities and an unquestioned power that is made available to them in God's Spirit. The gift of imagination is what takes them there.

In this chapter, I will explore what imagination has to do with spiritual formation. I hope you will come to understand, in a deeper way, how valuable the gift of imagination is. It not only fosters the development of your children's creative capacity, but it is absolutely necessary if they are ever to experience a feeling of empathy for another child. It is indeed a rich gift. But, in order to give imagination the time and attention needed to develop, you will need to look at your family's pace of life. When we are constantly running, we miss out on just being. We will never fully understand what is happening around us if we don't stop, slow down, and listen to what God is telling us. We can't know what any of life's mysteries mean unless we take the time to listen for what God is trying to teach us in the moments of our everyday lives. Our children, on the other hand, know how to listen to the silence and slow down so they can hear the "whisper across the heart" that is the voice of God.

IMAGINATIVE PLAY

We have all enjoyed watching children play imaginatively. I remember how wonderful it was to watch my young grandson play with the "pegs in the triangle" game that was provided for us on the table at a restaurant while we waited for our food to be served. He made up his own game using the pegs. The pegs were given names and definite roles to play and became animated with voices. He could play with those simple pegs indefinitely and did not suffer from boredom while he waited for his food. Still, at age fourteen, he can find amusement in almost any situation by using his imagination.

A young mother told me what happened with her three-year-old daughter after she saw a theatre production of Shakespeare's *A Midsummer Night's Dream*. The next day the mother and her daughter spent some leisurely time in the woods. Her daughter proceeded to gather sticks and stones and recreate the play right there in the woods. The mother sat and watched her play for at least an hour. Her daughter was totally immersed in her imaginative play. Today, at age fourteen, she is a stage actress and still finds God in the woods.

GIFT OF IMAGINATION

Judy Gattis Smith, a Christian educator, said this about the gift of imagination:

> Imagination can help us picture in the mind what is not apparent to the physical senses. It is the faculty by which we perceive what we have not observed by experience. Imagination gives us a haunting power over time. The joy of living fully through our senses is preserved for us by our own ability to duplicate them in our imaginations. We savor life, tasting and retasting, seeing and reseeing through imagination. Imagination can give us strength for Christian living by helping us postpone satisfaction, denying ourselves for the sake of others, believing in the existence of what cannot be seen, giving us hope for eternal life. Imagination has great power to change lives by giving us personal insights. Fantasy can bring about renewed energy and a renewed capacity for achieving inner serenity.[1]

---

1. Smith, *Teaching to Wonder: Spiritual Growth Through Imagination and Movement,* 17.

The Role of Imagination in Spiritual Formation

This capacity for imagination is inherent in all humans. It can be fostered and encouraged. By the time a child is eighteen months old, and sometimes before, children show signs of make-believe in their play. Any item has the potential for becoming most anything they want it to. I was reminded of this as my daughter told me what her nine-month-old son had discovered. He had found a new use for his four new teeth. He scraped his new teeth over the rounded end of the glazed spout on a ceramic watering can, making a grating racket that was amplified in the body of the watering can. It was very loud and irritating to his parents, but he loved to do it. I wonder if the moment he discovered he could make a sound on something that looked a little like his parents' instruments (they are both professional musicians), he imagined he was playing an instrument too. Their horns have mouthpieces and bells that reverberate with sound. He was very familiar with the sounds since he had heard them his entire life—in the womb and out. The sound he made is not beautiful to his parents' ears, but to him, it had appeal.

His imagination worked overtime in those early months as he tested and tried objects in myriad ways in order to make sense of them and find new ways to use them. It took time to explore, to let go of preconceived ideas, and to look completely at "what is" and "what could be." When a child plays they are living in "kairos," or God's time. It is only in kairos that we can become what we were meant to be as human beings, participating with God in the wonder of His creation.

VALUING THE CHILD'S IMAGINATION

Children's imaginations develop out of an infant's capacity for emotional relationships. It is not an intellectual function. As children interact with caregivers, they come to identify with the thoughts and experiences of others. Then they are able to take alternative roles or positions, which are involved in pretend play and extending empathy to others.

Out of a child's ability to imagine comes an adult's capacity for the development of compassion. If you think about it, it makes perfect sense that one has to be able to feel something for another person in order to express compassion. We cannot experience or feel empathy unless we have the capacity to put ourselves in another's place. It helps to have experienced the same thing, but if we haven't, our imaginations become very useful in helping us imagine what it would be like. When we experience love for God, ourselves, and our families, we then can offer it to others. We know it is good and want others to experience it as well.

THE DEVELOPING IMAGINATION

Young children spend the majority of their days actively using their imaginations in everything they do. They have no preconceived ideas about the way to use the "stuff" our homes are full of until they are shown how to use something. There are limitless possibilities for any item they might encounter. After a baby has looked at, tasted, and chewed on an item that is new to them, he or she might decide it is useful for something none of us would have thought of. After all, nothing is impossible in their world.

This kind of imaginative play helps children transform themselves and their lives. All they need is a simple moment of silence to look inside themselves to find a whole new world where they can be anyone or anything they want to be. I watch my two-and-a-half-year-old granddaughter enter the world of the princess. She lives, breathes, and even sleeps in that world.

Using their imagination doesn't always have to be a mental process. It can take the form of music, dancing, art, or even storytelling, to name a few. Children need time to daydream, to let the mind wander, to let a box or clean piece of paper rest with them until it becomes a playhouse or a train or a painting in their mind. Creating something from nothing or from an object dissimilar to that which it becomes requires time to explore, to make changes, or to play randomly with the materials. Expanding the imagination requires practice. How much time do we give our children to daydream and explore without other demands?

Paul Harris from the Harvard Graduate School of Education has written a book titled *The Work of the Imagination*. In this book he discusses how we use our imagination to make judgments about how things might have been different if we had done something another way. We ask ourselves what went wrong or what we could have done better. In doing so, we are exercising our imagination.

Harris reminds us that we also use our imagination when we listen to a story or read a book and build a mental image of the situation that is being described. As it turns out, it is that mental image we keep over a long period of time rather than the words that were spoken or written. Our ability to do this comes from the years we practiced doing it as a young child in our pretend play. Imaginative play enabled us to think about another time or place far removed from the one we occupied at the moment.

Scripture gives us some marvelous examples of situations that seem so magical or mysterious that we might consider them a work of the imagination instead of fact. I think any adult would have a difficult time imagining that he or she really could walk on water. The disciple, Peter, struggled with that concept even as he was actually doing it. He took his eyes off of Jesus and slipped back into his known reality and sunk. On the contrary, author Madeleine L'Engle believed as a child that she floated down the long stairway in her home without ever touching her feet to the floor. No one told her she couldn't do it, and she knows she did it. Who can argue with that?

In the early elementary years, a child, who was previously applauded for imaginative stories, is now expected to live with a sense of reality and truth. What was really cute as a toddler ceases, for some, to be an attribute to be nurtured. After all, a parent wants to foster truth-telling. At this age a child's use of imagination and fantasy can be misconstrued as lies or stretching of the truth. In my years as a children's pastor, parents came to me concerned that their children could not separate fantasy from reality. Many think it is time to move out of this stage into concrete thinking, when in reality, a healthy imagination is one of the most important tools for problem solving and for developing compassion and empathy. When we ask children to deal with problems beyond their cognitive abilities, understanding, and control, they can become anxious, tune out, and develop a disassociation from the issues. Rather than snuffing out imaginative play, it needs to be nurtured.

DETRIMENTS TO THE DEVELOPMENT OF THE IMAGINATION

There are several factors that negatively affect the development of the imagination. For many children the time outside of school is taken up by structured activities that leave no room for imaginative play. Children need "slow time," yet so many parents seem to be afraid of letting their children get bored. There is a common belief that says activities are good for a child. I wish more parents would choose to let their children be bored, which might in turn help them learn how to self-entertain.

This would be good for the parents as well as the children. Imagine yourself being unstructured with a day or a portion of a day to do nothing. For most, that would feel peaceful.

The amount of time spent in school is another one of those factors. It has increased several hours since 1989. Children's playtime, on the other hand, has decreased by twenty-five percent. Also, play environments have changed from neighborhood natural areas to plastic, wood, and metal playgrounds and structured sports activities. While none of this is bad, it is so much better for children when they can play in natural environments. Outside, their play is more diverse, with imaginative and creative play that fosters language and collaborative skills. Charlotte Mason, an originator of home school curriculums, recommends that it would be good for children to spend six hours out of their day playing, and it would be best if most of it was spent outdoors.

BENEFITS OF OUTDOOR PLAY FOR THE IMAGINATION

Outdoor play helps buffer the life stress on children. It helps them deal with all those things that go wrong in their young lives. The more time they spend outdoors, the more they benefit. When children play outside, they develop powers of observation and creativity. They are more peaceful and in sync with the world, and it can help reduce or eliminate the bullying that plagues children on playgrounds. Natural environments stimulate social interaction between children and they develop more positive feelings about each other.

Early experiences with nature have been positively linked with the development of imagination and the sense of wonder, which is a form of worship. Empathy and compassion as well as independence and autonomy are all fostered in the wonderful world of cooperative play, particularly in nature. All of this contributes to their spiritual formation. God is present in all of His created order, and children need to be exposed to Him in that realm as much, if not more, than within the walls that house so much of their spiritual lives.

When children grow up playing outside, they naturally notice nature. They may try to find the hugest tree or look at all the veins in a large leaf. They observe how hard ants work and how bright the colors are on some birds. It makes it so much easier for them to imagine how big or clever God is.

The Role of Imagination in Spiritual Formation

RETAINING THE IMAGINATION

After recognizing the value of the imagination, how do we help children retain their imagining ability into their adult years? I believe that practicing the following principles will help keep the imaginative ability alive and functioning:

1. Teach children to ask "what if?" questions. Considering alternatives will stimulate inventive or imaginative thinking.

2. Encourage them to talk out loud about what happened when they find themselves in frustrating situations. It is good to try and figure out what went wrong.

3. Bring your children into your problem solving. For example, when you are working in the kitchen or the garage, you can introduce them to invention. Let them try some things. Take their suggestions and see how they work. Compare one idea to another. Play the "what if?" game with them while you are cooking or repairing something. Talk out loud while you work through your brainstorming process so they can hear how you think while you work.

4. Build something or make something from scratch that you have written about or drawn down on paper. They will have opportunity to see how a project moves from vision to reality. Your children can experience the joy of realizing a vision that didn't come from someone else's plan.

5. Let them see that you are not afraid to make a mistake. Sometimes making up stories or songs, even if you don't sing on pitch will show them that everyone can try.

6. Stimulate and nurture your children's imagination. Let them dream wild, imaginative dreams of good winning over evil. Encourage them to think about transforming some common ordinary thing into something truly amazing and marvelous. This kind of exercise will help ensure that they will be able to experience a lifetime of invention and imaginative happenings.

7. Encourage them to dream visions of what might be. This is necessary if they ever want to solve problems or create something

significant. Who knows? Maybe you have a prophet in your household!

8. Play open-ended games and activities with them. I remember fondly the games my friends and I invented in our backyards. They provided hours of imaginative, healthy play. With so much structured activity, children often have to conform to staying within the rules of the game instead of making up their own. When they create their own, they find out what works and what doesn't.

9. Allow children to be really silly at times. Discovery of nonsense jokes and silly stories results in gales of laughter and fun. Challenge them to make the craziest pizza, for instance.

10. Do not overschedule your child. While classes and training can be good and stimulating to your child, anything that prevents inventiveness or adaptation is to be avoided.

11. Choose videos and television programs that provide enriching visual stimulation. Limit the amount of time spent, however, because the child is only a spectator.

12. Stay involved with your child around the content of the TV selections by talking about the program during and after viewing it together.

13. Spend time together outside. Join them as they notice and wonder at the natural world. You might try sending them a little ways away and then call them back to tell you all about something they saw. See how much detail they can describe.

There are many reasons for cultivating the imagination. Beyond all else, using their imagination helps children become whole and responsible human beings, creating a life of vision, value, and meaning. Recapturing the innocence of childhood through imagination is both real and important. It gives us the chance to be with our children unencumbered by the stress of the material world. Taking this journey together, we become light, joyful, and free. What an extraordinary and heartening possibility.

The Role of Imagination in Spiritual Formation

IMAGINATION AND SPIRITUAL HUNGER

Maria Montessori refers to the imagination as something that feeds our *spiritual hunger*. She tells the story of a young school child who, after reading the Christmas story from the Bible, tells how the angels popped out of heaven when it opened. The telling of that story produced mental images of power, grandeur, and mystery. That power to produce images in our mind is one of the strengths of the imagination; without it, no faith or religion can really exist. We must imagine the invisible with our mind's eye. This power reminds me of the verse in Hebrews 11 that talks about "faith being the evidence of things unseen." We are capable of producing images in our minds of things that are eternal. Our response to life is different if we have been taught only a definition of faith than if we have trembled with Abraham as he held a knife over Isaac.

FANTASY AND THE MORAL IMAGINATION

J. R. R. Tolkein wrote an essay about fairy stories in which he discusses reason, the moral imagination, and truth. He believed fantasy is a natural and important activity that does not destroy reason. The clearer and keener reason is, the better the fantasy it will make. If we were to find ourselves in a place where we did not want to hear or understand truth, fantasy would languish until we were healed or cured.

Children do not find it difficult to distinguish between frogs and men in a fairy tale. Vigen Gurioan, a professor and author of *On Fairy Tales and the Moral Imagination,* says:

> Children find frog-princes interesting because they know themselves as incomplete and not entirely whole. And they are attracted to the story of *The Ugly Duckling* and *The Lame Prince* because reason tells them, based upon simple observation that they too are in some sense "handicapped" or disadvantaged with respect to adults. When children long for the day that they will be equal in strength and capacity to grown-ups, however, more than reason is at play. The imagination is at work. Children want and need to explore just what it might be like to turn out finally "whole" and all right, to be a good parent, or the best of rulers. In this respect *Pinocchio* is the quintessential child.
>
> And isn't this yearning to be whole and wholly real what also attracts even adults to fairy kings and queens who are not frogs, to *Prince Caspian* in C. S. Lewis's *Chronicles* or *Princess Irene* of

> George MacDonald's *The Princess and the Goblin*? These literary sub-creations possess the power to move the will far beyond what reason indicates. They feed the moral imagination and, finally, the religious sense of divine awe before divine mystery and reverence for what is good, beautiful, and true.[2]

Plato argues that conversion to what is right and good is like an *aha* moment when we remember something long forgotten. Our atrophied imaginations need to be brought back to life. Symbols, allegories, fables, myths, and great stories are perfect for doing this. They take us to a place where we can really see ourselves against a moral order and meaning that transcends this life.

When the struggle between good and evil is dramatically portrayed with characters who depict all the possibilities, our moral vision becomes clear. We experience light in our eyes, joy in our hearts, and brightness in our thinking. Fairy tales are neither scientific nor practical guides for living. They are full of examples of the very best human qualities and relationships to others. A world that respects the moral laws is depicted. When that law is broken, a heavy price is paid. They show us that there really is a difference between what is logically possible and what is morally permissible. The heroes in fairy tales, while free and responsible, are called upon to be respectful of the moral law.

After reading Hans Christian Andersen's *Snow Queen*, a child's moral imagination will most likely be sure to have been stimulated and sharpened. The original fairy tales do a better job of projecting powerful images of good and evil. They show dire consequences as well. A child can learn how to love through the examples of characters he or she has come to love and admire. These memories become part of a child's self-identity and character. They help a child make real-life decisions. When children's hearts and minds are full of rich story material, they move through their world with moral intent and, hopefully, with faith, hope, and love.

EXERCISING THE ADULT IMAGINATION

The use of imagination is not just for children. There are so many positive outcomes for adults who continue to activate their imagination in living life with God themselves and with their families. Judy Gattis Smith, who wrote *Teaching to Wonder: Spiritual Growth Through Imagination*

---

2. Gurioan, *On Fairy Tales and the Moral Imagination*, 23.

and Movement, said that use of the imagination gives us a sense of power over time. As adults, we are called to live in kairos. We find our sense of being and dream dreams that are not bound by time or space. Peter, from the New Testament Gospels, thought he was dreaming when the angels unlocked the gates and led him out of prison. Madeleine L'Engle says that if we pay attention to our angels, we will find that the dream world and the waking world are not as far apart as we might think. Sometimes we move through the ages, everywhere, and even sometimes beyond this world. We can soar and fly. I believe we were meant to fly on eagles' wings, as stated in scripture.

We can live life fully through our senses and relive moments by imagining them in our minds. We can feel, taste, and see through the use of our imagination. It can give us strength for living by helping us delay satisfaction, deny ourselves for the sake of others, and believe in what cannot be seen by our physical eyes—all of which gives us hope for eternal life. We gain personal insights through the use of our imaginations, which can bring about change in our lives. Fantasy, on the other hand, can bring new energy to life and a capacity for experiencing peace.

Our minds, as adults, are full of pictures from our past and present. Some of them are lovely, and some are horrific. I am reminded of what Jesus said to His disciples at a time when they were pretty distressed about what was happening to Him. He told them to "return to Galilee." There they would find Him again as they relived in their minds the life they had had with Him. Returning to Galilee enabled them to walk the roads and remember what He had taught and lived before them. They saw Him in their minds' eye and felt His presence.

Slowing down enough to remember where you have been with God enables you to revisit those moments and places that have been life changing or significant. Anthony DeMello, who writes about Eastern spiritual practices in his book, *Sadhana, A Way to God*, invites us to return in our imagination to some scene where we experienced God's goodness and God's love for us. He suggests that we stay in that place and take in the love of God once again. Then we are to return to the present moment and have a conversation with God. He goes on to say that it is most important that we relive the moment, not just remember it. Through reliving it, we will once again feel the feelings we experienced then, such as joy, intimacy, love, or some other strong emotion. He cautions that we do not run away from these feelings but stay in that place until we feel peaceful and content. Then, we can return to the present and have another conversation with God.

A LIFE-CHANGING EXPERIENCE

DeMello's exercise reminded me of one of my life-changing experiences with God. I was attending a weekend silent retreat, the first I had ever been involved with. After being totally silent for two and a half days, we all went to the chapel for our final communion service together to break the silence before going home. I arrived a few minutes early and sat in the back row of the chapel in the Catholic retreat center, listening to soft guitar worship music. I was still and quiet and began to glance at the crucifixes that were mounted on the wall off to my right. As my eyes gazed at a statue, it was as if I saw God's love and felt it fall on me for the first time. I had always known intellectually that God loved me, but I had never felt loved or known by Him. In this moment, I understood on a deep and new level what He had done for me and felt His love burn deep into my heart. The dam in my heart broke open and I cried until I couldn't cry any more as I began to take it all in.

Until that time, I had always felt that there had to be more to this Christian life than I had experienced but I didn't know how to get it. One gaze on His statued face broke into my heart and flooded me with love that couldn't be denied. God used a statue, which had been forbidden in my particular Christian culture, to reach my longing heart in a new way. The doubt that had plagued me from childhood was gone. I knew His love for the very first time. It was so precious! I didn't even have words to express how I felt. I was overcome with love.

I can close my eyes and reenter that moment anytime I want or need to. It comes back to me in vivid color. The song "Amazing Grace" brings back the memory every time I hear it because it was the song being played at the time. I can still see myself sitting in the pew, sobbing my heart out. I left that experience, after sharing it with the other participants of the retreat, with a solid trust and belief that what I had experienced with God in the final moments of that weekend retreat was real. I have lived many years since that fateful moment and it is not any less real to me now than it was at that time.

Every one of you carries in your heart an album of lovely pictures from your past: memories of events that brought gladness to you. They are there for your use in those moments when you need to be reminded of God's goodness or of His love for you. I needed to recall and reenter my life-changing moment when I was experiencing my first MRI. Because they were scanning my head, I had to be completely enclosed inside the tube. Being a bit claustrophobic, I knew that undergoing the MRI was going to be a very difficult experience. With the help of a sedative, a blindfold, and a warm blanket, I went into the tube. I directed my mind to look into Jesus' face as I had done in that chapel so long ago. As I focused on Him, I felt loved and cared for, surrounded by his warm embrace. My terror and fear evaporated. The time slipped away without taking any break from the constant pounding of the machine as it did its work. God met my need and I got to enjoy His company while I lay there so very still.

Over time, the face of God changed for me. The face of God in my childhood memory was stern and full of eyes all around His head. After all, He was everywhere all the time and could see in every direction at the same time. There was no way to get away from the eye. He knew what I did and I never succeeded in getting away with anything without getting caught. I was convinced He and my parents worked quite closely together.

After the retreat experience, I saw eyes full of love and a smile on His face. His touch was gentle and inviting. I no longer feared His judgment, even though He had every right to judge me. His forgiveness was always available and the smile remained on His face when He looked at me.

During my years as a children's pastor, I spent time asking children questions about their picture of God. When I asked what God's face looked like when He looked at them, I heard all of them tell me He smiled at them. Some embellished it a bit and gave Him white hair, but most talked about His smile. What a different picture they had than the one I had grown up with! They were not afraid of God but wanted to be close to Him.

OPPOSITION TO THE USE OF THE IMAGINATION

I don't believe that the gift of imagination deserves the bad rap it gets in many Christian circles. Maybe the word *imagination* gets wrongly associated with the word *imaginary*. To some, imagination stands in opposition to reality. Haven't you heard the statement made, "You've got quite an imagination!" when someone doesn't believe the story they have just been told?

But God gave us our imagination, so surely it is not inherently evil. Jesus used his imagination when He used parables for teaching His followers. The stories were not about actual events but had been drawn from His life experience and imagination to teach eternal truths.

DREAMS AND IMAGINATION

Dreams come from our imagination while we sleep. In the Old Testament, God often spoke to prophets and others through dreams. The New Testament tells us how an angel of the Lord appeared in a dream to Joseph, telling him to take Mary and baby Jesus to safety in Egypt, and later in the same way told him when it was safe to return to Israel (Matthew 2:13 and 19). In Acts 2:17, we are told that in the last days when God pours out His Spirit, "your young men shall see visions and your old men dream dreams." In each of these instances, God took the initiative to bring about a dream for His specific purposes. Might He not also use our waking dreams for His purposes? Might we not, by the leading of the Holy Spirit, draw our own parable-like pictures to make real the Lord's presence in our lives to others? I think we can, and in fact, most of us probably already do.

We use our imaginations when we need to create a picture of something or relive a memory that we can't see with our eyes. Have you, in prayer, pictured Jesus standing with His hands outstretched toward you? At times of deep repentance have you pictured yourself kneeling at the foot of the cross or at His feet? In moments of praise, I have lifted my hands and voice to the lamb upon the throne.

USE OF THE IMAGINATION IN SCRIPTURE

Scripture has painted pictures with words for us that we can take into our minds to draw us more closely into the presence of Jesus. Throughout the history of the Church, hymn writers have blessed us with words and images that would reach our imaginations in ways that bring us more fully into the presence of the King. After all, the imagination is the eye of the heart. If our heart is set on that which is good and holy, it will draw us to the Lord. He tells us to set our minds on things that are above, not on things below. We are to think on whatever things are good and true. If we seek ungodly things, then our imagination will draw us to wrongdoing. The more of God's goodness we are able to capture in our imaginations,

The Role of Imagination in Spiritual Formation

the more resources we will have when we find ourselves tempted to look in the opposite direction.

A WORD TO PARENTS

As parents, we don't want to lose sight of the Creator in our children. They are bearers of His light and life. We have the privilege and honor of helping them remember and reconnect with Him by helping them see God in their everyday lives and world. You are a sacred connector, naming their experiences so that they can find Him for themselves.

You also have the divine privilege of nurturing their imagination so they can see with the "eyes of their heart"; so they can feel with others; so they can experience empathy and compassion; so they can love a God they cannot physically see with all their heart, their soul, and their might; so they can love others like they do themselves. He wants them to use their Holy imaginations.

Scottie May, a Christian educator, shared the story of Julie, a four-year-old who became captivated by the telling of the Passion story on Palm Sunday in the church she attended. As the little girl listened, she heard it as if it was happening right in front of her very eyes. It was so real to her. She saw and felt the suffering of Jesus. She hung on to every word she heard.

When the story ended, Julie continued to cry. In fact, her mother said she wept well into the afternoon. Her sense of justice and morality told her that Jesus' death was wrong, and it broke her heart to know He suffered so much. Julie had heard many times that Jesus loved her, but the thought of His death was too painful for her to bear.

Her parents tried their best to comfort her. They explained to Julie that, in fact, the people had just acted out the story that had happened so long ago. They assured her that the pastor was only an actor and that he was very much alive. They also told her the Easter story. Even though Jesus had been wrongly killed, on the third day God reached down and brought Jesus back to life. Her parents' words seemed to make her feel a little bit better. She wasn't easily persuaded, however, because she had seen the whole story of His death acted out before her. Julie's imagination was full of the pictures of that reenactment.

As the week progressed, the little girl began to act like herself again. Easter came and Julie attended church with her family. As the hymn "Jesus

Christ Is Risen Today" was sung, the pastor who had played the role of Jesus the week before walked down the aisle of the church. Julie spotted him and took off running. She ran to him, threw her arms around him, and cried, "It is true. You are alive. You are not dead anymore. God gave you back to us." Her parents arrived on the scene and gently led her back to her place in the pew. She was one happy girl. Easter was truly a glorious experience for her. Jesus was alive!

Jesus told His disciples that they were to let the children come to Him. They were not to stop them from coming because, after all, the Kingdom of God belongs to them. Julie entered the sacred story of Jesus through her Holy imagination.

Young children are capable of empathizing with characters in a story. Because of their sensitivities, it is important for parents to carefully choose the stories they share. As was stated in an earlier chapter, the stories need to meet a specific need for the child, preferably in their sensitive period for that truth. In telling the holy stories, we need to be absolutely convinced of their truth and that they are right for our child in that period of their development. We dare not err in this, because to a child, we speak with the voice of authority. Thankfully, God has not left us alone in this process. The Holy Spirit is there to guide us in all the choices we make on behalf of our children.

None of us are perfect parents or teachers. No one is perfectly wise. We don't always transmit moral truth well. We can't make our children good. But we can help them learn to love what is good. You can love them as perfectly as imperfect human beings are capable of doing. I believe that is what God asks us to do. When we love our children and help them use the God-given gift of imagination to help them in this life, we are, in fact, showing our love for Him as well.

QUESTIONS TO CONSIDER

1. When have you experienced the gift of holy imagination? Let yourself reenter that place and relive it again. How did it feel? Did anything change?

2. Think of a time you have directed your child to use their imagination to resolve or solve a problem. How did it work? Knowing what you know now, was there anything you would change?

3. What is God teaching you as you think about the ways imagination can be used in your life and that of your children?

10

Tools for Calming Fears and Healing Wounds

*A happy heart makes the face cheerful, but heartache crushes
the spirit. . . . A cheerful look brings joy to the heart,
and good news gives health to the bones.*

—PROVERBS 15:13, 30

I AM SURE THAT all parents would like their children to avoid fears that can paralyze and render them unable to trust God or others in their life. When fears take hold, they cause one to close up or shut down in a self-protective posture; just the opposite from the open-arms, open-heart posture that makes growth with God possible. Fears can also produce mental, emotional, and physical problems. That is why I have included this chapter. Children, as well as adults, need healing of wounds and fears that only God, in His divine care and mercy, can provide. Children can use some of the tools that you have already given them during combat with the Enemy. When they successfully do this, the life of God can grow and flourish in them.

Children are not the only ones to experience these kinds of fears. The disciples that were with Jesus through all kinds of harrowing experiences had fears as well. Max Lucado, the author of *The Eye of the Storm*, says:

> Biographies of bold disciples begin with chapters of honest terror. Fear of failure. Fear of loneliness. Fear of a wasted life. Fear of failing to know God. Faith begins when you see God on the mountain and you are in the valley and you know that you're too weak to make the climb. . . . Faith that begins with fear will end up nearer the Father.[1]

---

1. Lucado, *The Eye of the Storm*, 136–37.

It is inevitable that our children will suffer from and have to face the normal fears that develop in their younger years. There are so many kinds of fears: fear of abandonment, loud noises, the dark, falling, strangers, nightmares, doing wrong things, strange places and foods, and strange sounds, just to name a few. Some fears are more predominant at specific ages. We, as parents, must encourage children to seek the help they need in the right places and push through the fears, emerging victorious and strong.

HOW FEARS DEVELOP

Research reveals that children acquire fear in the following ways: conditioning, vicarious learning, and information transfer. Conditioned fear develops in response to something frightening happening in the presence of a previously neutral object. For example, being chased by a puppy may trigger the child to become fearful of dogs. A child who sees that someone else is scared of something can develop fears. This is called vicarious learning. Watching a parent scream at the sight of spiders may suggest that these critters are scary.

Rabbi Noach Orlowek shares the following story about the acquisition of a fear of ants by a three-year-old girl. Her parents couldn't figure out why their daughter suddenly became frightened of ants. After thinking about it for a while, they discovered that two days before, the child's aunt had found some ants in the kitchen and said, "Oh no, look at the ants in here! They'll eat up absolutely everything." What the young girl interpreted from this was that "everything" included her.

All of us inadvertently cause fear when we react strongly to something we don't like or are afraid of. Becoming aware of that in a situation that poses potential threats to your child's security can help an adult avert the possibility of "passing a fear on" to your child. If you are able to be calm and positive, your children will model your behavior in their response to the situation.

The following story is a good example of that. During the Gulf War in Israel, the sirens went off to let everyone know that missiles were coming in from Iraq. Everyone was supposed to run off to the room specifically sealed against a possible gas attack. One family had their daughter's friend visiting with them when one of the attacks began. The father had to quickly decide if the girl should stay with his family or go back to her

Tools for Calming Fears and Healing Wounds

parent's home in the next block. He didn't know if the civil defense would approve, but he chose to bring her home so she could be with her family.

While they walked to her home, the streets were empty as the sirens blared. The child knew very well what the sirens meant, but she wasn't afraid, because the father wasn't afraid. Children often reflect how we feel.

When we tell someone that something is dangerous and should be feared, it sometimes results in information transfer. Studies show that information about what is scary may play an important role in the development of fears and phobias. For instance, when careless adults tell ghost stories to young children, they sometimes create images of monsters and begin to fear.

TWO NATURAL FEARS

Scientists tell us that humans are born with only two fears, both of which are natural instincts: loud noises and falling. If you have observed babies you know they jump at loud, startling noises. Think about the environment they have just come from, where sounds were muted as they traveled to the baby deep inside the mother's womb. Babies are also fearful of falling. They are used to fitting so snuggly inside the womb. There is not much room to move, and their arms are tightly pressed against their bodies. Carried in that kind of environment for so many months, they were protected from falling and they could constantly feel the parts of their body against the inside of the mother's protective womb.

Out of that environment babies are totally dependent on someone to hold them tightly and carefully so they don't feel the open space around them so keenly. What an act of trust it is to finally let go of furniture or a parent's finger and stand alone, not dependent on anyone or anything. Then they finally take those first steps toward independent walking for the first time. Those steps signify a huge change for a child, and they are often preceded by some helpful games played with parents. Playing games of 'toss in the air" while a parent catches them helps build confidence. A building block of trust established earlier creates an environment where risk is minimized because there are loving parents around to catch and protect them.

OTHER COMMON FEARS

Children between the ages of two and six usually experience many more fears than adults because of their small size and the knowledge that they are powerless. They also lack the ability to understand the world around them. But this enables them to ask for help more easily because they are not embarrassed or ashamed to do so. This is one of the characteristics of young children that Jesus recognized and acknowledged when he rebuked his disciples in front of the large crowd that had gathered to hear him speak in Galilee.

It is very normal for children to have particular fears at certain ages. It is helpful for parents to expect them. Here are some of the most common fears:

- Six months to two years: fear of separation, strangers, baths, loud noises, and falling
- Two to four years: fear of animals, storms, dark, people in masks or costumes, doctors, and toilets
- Four years: fear of ghosts and monsters
- Five to six years: realistic fears of leaving home, going to school, and burglars and other "bad" people
- Eight years and older: fear of death, bullies, ridicule from peers, principals and teachers, divorce or separation from parents, and getting lost

There are some strange fears that are less common but are frequently seen enough to have acquired actual names. Some of the ones that might affect children are:

- Achluophobia: fear of darkness
- Arachybutyrophobia: fear of peanut butter sticking to the roof of the mouth
- Aviophobia: fear of flying
- Brontophobia: fear of thunder and lightning
- Clinophobia: fear of going to bed
- Helmintophobia: fear of worm infestation

Tools for Calming Fears and Healing Wounds

- Hemophobia: fear of blood
- Ophidiophobia: fear of snakes
- Sciophobia: fear of shadows

It is not difficult to understand how these fears develop if we place ourselves in a child's shoes. Imagine for a moment that you are eighteen months to two years old, are not very tall, and have a limited understanding of how the world operates. Then place yourself in the following situations:

- I hear a thunderstorm outside.
- The toilet flushes and I watch all the water as it goes down the toilet.
- I am standing in the middle of a crowded elevator.
- A huge dog jumps on me.
- My parents' friends, whom I've never met, pick me up and hug and kiss me.
- While in a dark room by myself, I see the wind blowing tree branches outside my window, making shadows that move on my wall.

By understanding that their fears reflect their intelligence and understanding of how the world works, it is easier to help children deal with their fears.

HOW PARENTS FACE FEARS

As I stated earlier, adults as well as children have fears. I remember an event from my early childhood that was the beginning of a fear it has taken me a lifetime to conquer. My parents took me to a circus performance. We sat way up at the top of the circus tent. I can still envision how far it was to the floor of the tent.

One of the acts was the balancing clown act. The clowns stacked many chairs on top of the other and then climbed to the top of the chairs in order to sit on the very highest chair. I can remember how that tower bent from side to side while the clown on top tried to keep his balance. I could see the danger in all of that. Falling was the natural consequence of the clowns' predicament in my young mind, and I did not want the clown to get hurt. I cried, screamed, and wanted them to stop. It absolutely terrified me then, and I still can feel that fear today.

As a result, anything up high, that was not solid or stable, continued to bother me into my adult years. Bridges, high buildings, elevators on the sides of buildings, cable cars, ski lifts, etc., almost paralyzed me with fear. Climbing on simple bleachers would make me dizzy. It was awful. I tried to walk over a very deep canyon on a bridge that had cracks between the boards and felt sick. So sick, in fact, that I had to get down on my hands and knees and crawl off of it. It was then that I knew I needed help with this phobia. It took facing my fear in a variety of ways to get over it. I rode ski lifts many times in a row until I was convinced it was safe. I would stand on high places while holding on to someone so that I wouldn't get hurt if I lost my balance.

I invited God into those experiences with me and I imagined holding on to Him. I knew He could be trusted to remain stable and secure when it felt like the ground was falling away from under me. I said His name and looked into His eyes. He held me in that gaze, and gradually the fear dissipated. I can ride a ski lift now or a cable car without unreasonable fear. In fact, I most often really enjoy it.

My children knew about the fear I had and tried to help me through it. It became important for me to tell them I was going for help. And they saw and experienced the results of that fear being conquered. They needed to see me become dependent on God to bring me out of my phobia because I couldn't do it for myself. My hope in letting my children in on the process was that they would find their courage in God as well. I hoped my example of turning to Him in need would give them permission to do the same with their fears. I know of no other real and lasting solution to overcoming irrational fears.

COMING BEFORE GOD WITH OUR FEARS

We have all experienced fear and must become aware of it to get through it and overcome it. The Bible often tells us to place our trust in God because He will protect us. It is an important choice to make. However, if we are not aware of our fear, we cannot make this choice to trust God, and so we stay further away. When we acknowledge our fear, we get in touch with our need for others and God. We can pray and ask God to make us aware of things such as a fear that we may be ignoring. The guilt and shame we feel about our past behaviors may inhibit our ability to conduct a thorough inventory. David prayed, "Search me, O God, and know my heart; test me and know my anxious thoughts. See if there is any offensive way in me, and lead me in the way everlasting" (Psalm 139:23–24).

In Romans 8:15, we read, "You haven't received the spirit of slaves that leads you into fear again. Instead, you have received the spirit of God's adopted children by which we call out, 'Abba! Father!'" That is good news. God loves to hear us cry out for Him. As I stated earlier, one of His favorite words that can come out of our mouths is "Help!" The Psalms are full of David's cries for deliverance from the things that made him so fearful. God provided him with what was needed to overcome them.

WAYS TO HELP OUR CHILDREN CONQUER THEIR FEARS IN A GODLY WAY

I have summarized the following suggestions that came from Anne Marie Robichaud, a staff writer for Canadian Parents Online:

1. Take your children's fears seriously. Listen and help them differentiate between reality and fantasy. It is so easy to make light of scary situations children find themselves in. A statement like "that's silly, there's nothing to be afraid of in the dark" is not helpful. Instead, use statements like "I know you are afraid of the dark. Now, let's see what we can do to help you feel better at bedtime."

    When dealing with fears of monsters or ghosts, let your children check under the bed and in closets with a flashlight. It is important not to join your children in their fears by sweeping monsters out from under their bed but to allow them to check and assure themselves that monsters exist only in their mind. Working with children to find solutions will give them comfort at the same time it gives them a measure of control over it.

2. Find the source of their fear. We can ask God to help us find the source of our children's particular fear at the time it is being experienced. Often, just knowing where the sound came from or what made the shadow on the wall will dissipate the debilitating fear. A father told me a story about his experience with his son last

Christmas: "Our little boy thought he heard a monster scratching his bedroom window. After a little investigation, we realized that it was the wind blowing a holiday wreath on the window! Once we identified the source, the fear went away."

Other times you may need to really listen to the child's words to hear what is said. Finding out exactly what they are afraid of will help you take steps to alleviate the problem. For example, if a child says he is afraid of the dark, but you find out he is actually afraid of the things he thinks he sees in his closet when the doors are open, this gives you information that you can do something about. Determining exactly what the problem is before putting the child to bed helps you take steps to help them beat their fears.

3. Minimize television viewing. Young children are more sensitive to images and sounds than we are. Even cartoons can be very scary for a young child. My grandchildren have experienced nightmares because they watched scary cartoons before going to bed. If this is the case, make sure your child understands that cartoons are not real and consider banning television programs that trigger fear in your child. It might be helpful to allow your children to turn off the television when they feel that the show is too scary. It gives them a measure of control.

    It's also important to avoid watching the news when your younger children are around. The news is geared toward an adult audience, not children, and often contains graphic stories about violence and human tragedy that children will find very disturbing. This can be especially upsetting before bedtime.

    I remember the time my three-year-old grandson started having nightmares. Sharks were a recurring theme in his dreams, and we found out he had seen *Jaws* before going to bed one night. It took years of talking it through with him before the nightmares stopped.

4. Read stories, both secular and sacred, that can help a child deal with fears cognitively. Reading the stories written specifically for the purpose of calming fears can help some children. Another way to help is to tell your own stories about how you conquered

Tools for Calming Fears and Healing Wounds

fear. Knowing that someone they love has had the same experience can go a long ways to help them overcome theirs.

5. Avoid using force. Conquering a fear of the dark takes time for a child. So it is best not to push them into facing their fears. For example, don't force your child to stay in his room with the door closed at bedtime or use his bedroom as a place for a timeout. This will sometimes worsen the situation. Give children a chance to deal with their fears one small step at a time. Continue to provide lots of reassurance and comfort, and hopefully, you will soon see a big difference.

6. Give your child some of your adult strength. Move in close to them, holding them or putting your arms around them. I would encourage them to imagine Jesus, as the Good Shepherd, putting His warm arms around them because that is what He loves to do.

7. Ask the child what you can do. Let them know you want to help make the experience less frightening. If they are afraid in an elevator, they may want you to hold them up high.

8. Talk about the frightening event. Help them know it is okay to be afraid, that you have fears too, and when you were little you were afraid of similar things. Let them know that even though they are afraid now, it does not mean they will always be afraid. Remind them to think of the fears they have already mastered.

9. Prepare children for experiences that they fear. This will help them manage the situation when they get to the place where the fear occurs. This approach respects your child, instead of making him or her feel ashamed for being afraid. It helps children work through their fears and gain mastery over their irrational responses.

10. Plan some fun activities that can be introduced to help alleviate some of the specific fears mentioned that are common to our children. Play is a nonstressful way to help them deal with new situations or help alleviate fears. It is a way for children to practice life skills in a fun setting. One method of mastering fears is called extinction. It is a behavior modification method that pairs

a fear with something pleasant. This reduces the ability of the event or situation to cause fear.

Some ways you could use extinction to help your child deal with a fear of the dark might be to play games with flashlights in a darkened room, show a family video or a movie in a darkened room, eat dinner by candlelight, stage a toy hunt by flashlight in a room with the lights dimmed, take a nighttime walk to look at the stars, or make shadow hand creatures on the wall.

The use of dramatic play is another way to help your children master their fear. If they are scared of going to the doctor, play doctor with them. Use various items from around the house or toy medical kits to help them understand what the doctor will be doing to them. Art materials can be used to help your children create what they are afraid of. Children can draw a picture of the doctor, the dentist, or the barber to help alleviate their fear of those situations.

11. Encourage the use of their "holy" imagination. If they have already had experience imagining Jesus active and alive in their life, the gift of "holy" imagination can work wonders to bring healing of the fear. Encourage children to close their eyes and look for Jesus' face. Ask children what they see and what Jesus wants them to do with their fear. Listen to their response and encourage them to do just what He says. When children are finished and open their eyes, remind them of the availability of Jesus anytime they need Him.

12. Pray with your children. They need to know that God is always available and wants to help them overcome their fears. Pray for your children. The prayers of parents on behalf of their children are powerful.

13. When nothing else works, consult an expert. It may be wise to seek a professional's advice if your child's fears are interfering with family activities, creating problems in making friends, creating an excuse for not going to school, and disrupting normal sleep habits. Although most childhood fears are not a reason for concern, parents should seek help for the child in order for

Tools for Calming Fears and Healing Wounds

them to cope with the challenging task and to aid in conquering the fear.[2]

On the positive side of things, fear gives children an opportunity to confront and master a potentially dangerous situation. Provide your children with a safe environment, opportunities to help them confront their fears, and tools to use. As a parent you'll feel better about letting them work it out. If you have helped them find Jesus as their source, they will know what to do in the most troubling of situations, and you will not be plagued with worry. Troubles will come, but God is bigger than all of them!

HEALING WOUNDS

It is natural for parents to try to protect their children from the tough bumps and bruises of life that inevitably happen to all human beings. The wounds that come feel more negative than positive. It is so difficult to stand by a child in pain and deal with the consequences of the wounding. Wounding comes in so many forms and can be so damaging to any part of a child's being.

Because of what parents experienced themselves in their developing years, they are inclined to try to protect their children from experiencing the same things that threatened them. That is a noble cause. But the truth is that no parent can protect their child completely, nor would it be wise for them to try to do so. A child must learn how to deal with the hurts that come and let the scabs form, making the child more resilient and strong.

The question that I often hear from parents is "how do I find the balance between overprotective intervention and careless neglect?" And then, "what can I do to help my child heal and grow stronger? What skills can children develop to be part of their own healing process as they mature?" Fearfulness and the experience of being wounded are part of our children's experience from the beginning of their life. This whole process of calming fears and healing wounds is part of a parent's job from the start. Once again, a parent is not alone in this job, even if he or she is a single parent. God wants to provide the help and wisdom you need to do your part well.

---

2. Robichaud, "Conquering those nighttime anxieties," lines 16–42.

Prebirth Wounds

There are many kinds of wounds we can think of that might befall our child after birth. But what about those wounds that happen while they are living in their mother's womb? Is it possible to receive healing for those wounds as well? I believe it is very possible once you become aware of the potential for healing and the resources available to you.

I can't imagine what it would be like to remember my life in my mother's womb; or to remember the woundedness I received there. Some people actually do remember parts of that life and have described it in great detail. I was amazed as I listened to a man tell me what he remembered of his own birth. He remembers the pressure of being pushed through the birth canal and his emergence into a cold room with blinding white light. His memories are not pleasant ones.

For some, life in the uterus is a safe place, perfectly designed and healthy; ready for all that is to take place during the nine-month period of development and growth. Parents can provide a nurturing support system for the baby during his or her development. A mother's diet and habits need to be healthy in order to foster optimum growth and development. Parents know the God of creation and wait for the baby's birth with a sense of wonder and awe. Then the baby feels wanted and welcomed. Their sense of "being" and "well-being" is intact.

For others, life in the womb is hellish. Poor diet, detrimental habits that affect the baby and the mother, attempted abortions, and the influx of rejection and abandonment hormones affect the baby's sense of "being" and "well-being." Even the lack of nurturing support systems is harmful to the baby's development. These are but a few of the possible detriments to the child's formation. Consequently, the cells carry the memory of many negative influences into the baby's new life after birth.

What happens to all those memories? Why do some people remember aspects of their prenatal life and others have no conscious memory of it at all? Thomas Armstrong, who has a PhD in human development, believes that the pituitary hormone, oxytocin, secreted by the mother and possibly by the baby at birth, not only stimulates contractions but also causes amnesia of the prebirth and birthing experiences. The memories are still tucked away in the cells of the baby's body but are no longer part of the conscious memory. It is likely that babies whose mothers secrete more oxytocin at the time of birth experience more amnesia than those who lack the hormone in sufficient strength to cause the baby to forget the conscious life in the mother's uterus. This helps explain why some people remember parts of their birth experience and others don't. It also explains why the mother forgets enough of the experience so that she is willing to go through subsequent births.

If a parent who has adopted a child knows a child has suffered from a difficult birth, abandonment, or separation from a parent at birth for any number of reasons, a prayer for healing the sense of being and well being can be prayed over the child. You can invite someone to pray for your child or do it yourself. A simple prayer might include the following elements:

- Thank God for the gift of the child into your home.
- Acknowledge the physical or emotional damage that you know or suspect exists from damage that occurred in the early years of the child's life.
- Name the hurts, wounds, or fears that may plague the child and ask God to bring healing to those wounded places, known or unknown.
- Pray for restoration of the child's sense of self and security.
- While praying, parents or community members who are present might be invited to touch the child gently or extend hands toward him or her while the prayer is being prayed. Anointing with oil, which symbolizes and acknowledges God's presence, would be appropriate at this time.

It is possible that this kind of praying for a child might need to be repeated over time in order to continue the healing process. Healing sometimes happens gradually rather than instantly.

THE USE OF THE HOLY IMAGINATION FOR HEALING

When a child suffers a physical ailment, it is possible for them to focus their thinking on the area that is hurting and imagine Jesus touching it and calming the pain or healing it. Jerome Berryman, who wrote *Children and the Theologians: Clearing the Way for Grace,* said that "children can be a means of grace when there is sickness and when there is death by their very presence and touching. . . . What they need is to be completely recognized as one of those who cares and can help care."[3] When I was very ill and bedridden at my daughter's home, her four-year-old son would often climb up on the bed with me to soothe and comfort me. I directed him a few times to hold his hands over my painful area and ask God to heal it. I could feel the warmth that came from his little hands and imagined God's mighty work in my healing process. From that point on, he would use his hands on his own body and on mine and would turn his mind to God for healing. I needed to explain to him that sometimes we can't see the healing going on, but it is happening just the same. Most often, when he used this tool to help himself, the pain would diminish quite quickly.

We talked about the fact that sometimes hurts don't go away right away, but he could ask Jesus to be with him during the hurting time. That seemed to calm him right away. His mind and heart had no trouble embracing this concept, and he sincerely believed. The holy imagination is a very useful tool for aiding the healing process of all kinds of wounds and fears. And children can easily access it anywhere and anytime.

There is tremendous healing power inherent in the process of using one's imagination to visualize health instead of illness. Fran Greenfield, an author who writes about the spiritual life, tells the story of a six-year-old girl who suffered from severe asthma. She had watched her mother use imagery as part of her healing from ovarian cancer and had learned to use it herself.

During one of her asthma attacks, she imagined entering her body to find out what got in the way of her breathing. Once inside, she saw that the sun and the moon were having a fight, so she joined with the sun to overcome the moon. Soon the battle was won and she felt relief. For the next seven days, she repeated the exercise and, amazingly, the asthmatic symptoms vanished. Since then, she has not needed to use her conventional medication for her asthma. Greenfield says she has seen many children overcome asthma using imagery techniques, and the benefits are much more than just relief of symptoms.

Using imagery requires patience and the time to just be. One must turn toward the pain and discomfort with Jesus instead of moving away from it. Using this kind of technique for life means children can connect to something greater than their own self-interest and to relate to their

---

3. Berryman, *Children and the Theologians*, 253–54.

hearts as well as their heads. It means unplugging from the noise and busyness of this life.

DEALING WITH SERIOUS LOSSES

Serious losses can wound children profoundly. In a small group experience for children who had suffered loss, the small group leader talked to them about Jesus' love for them. He told them that God's love was like a warm blanket wrapped tightly around them. No harm could come to them when they were wrapped tightly in His loving arms. The leader rolled each child, one by one, in a warm blanket and held them in the blanket for a short time. Then they were told that Jesus loved them so much and was available to comfort them anytime they needed it. They could even roll up in their own blankets at home and imagine Jesus holding and comforting them.

The children loved the experience so much that they asked for it often during the remaining sessions. I also heard from parents that their children had been asking to be wrapped in a blanket at home. Some even did it by themselves and received the comfort it brought. The cry of the child often is to "do it by myself," and having some skills to do so can be very empowering. They need to know that God is the One who is most available to help them when they aren't feeling good in their body or spirit. Unless they know He loves to help them, they will find other things to help take away the pain.

What it all comes down to is that Jesus is the answer for our lives and our children's lives. He was the one who taught His disciples to do what He did: heal the sick, raise the dead, cleanse the lepers, and cast out demons (Matthew 10:8). Through the power of the Holy Spirit we can bring peace to our children's fearful hearts and healing to their minds, bodies, and spirits. They will learn to do likewise because they have learned from you. The Holy Spirit is as available to them as He is to you. He will give them what they need to calm fears and bring healing for themselves and others. And so we join with others through the ages and say the words of the Gloria Patri: "Glory be to the Father, and to the Son, and to the Holy Spirit; as it was in the beginning, is now and ever shall be, world without end. Amen."

QUESTIONS TO CONSIDER

1. What fears affect your life on a regular basis?
2. What have you done in the past about situations where you were seized with fear?
3. Where is God when you are feeling fearful?
4. What things do you need to change in order to overcome the fears that plague you?
5. What fears have your children experienced?
6. How can you best help your children overcome their fears?
7. What woundedness have you dealt with in your own life?
8. How have your children been wounded?
9. What techniques might you try to help them heal and grow strong in spite of the wounds?
10. What might hold you back from trusting God in new ways?

Appendix A

THE GOOD SHEPHERD PARABLE

John 10

For Young Children

(3b) The Good Shepherd calls his own sheep by name and leads them out.

(4) When he has brought out all his own, he goes ahead of them, and the sheep follow him because they know his voice.

(5) They will not follow a stranger, but they will run from him because they do not know the voice of strangers.

(10b) I came that they may have life, and have it abundantly.

(11) I am the good shepherd. The good shepherd lays down his life for the sheep.

(14) I am the good shepherd. I know my own and my own know me,

(15) just as the Father knows me and I know the Father. And I lay down my life for the sheep.

(16) I have other sheep that do not belong to this fold. I must bring them also, and they will listen to my voice. So there will be one flock, one shepherd.

Appendix A

For Older Children

Include the following verses from John and Luke as well:

> (12) The hired hand, who is not the shepherd and does not own the sheep, sees the wolf coming and leaves the sheep and runs away and the wolf snatches them and scatters them.

> (13) The hired hand runs away because a hired hand does not care for the sheep.

FOUND SHEEP PARABLE

Luke 15

> (4) Which one of you, having a hundred sheep and losing one of them, does not leave the ninety-nine in the wilderness and go after the one that is lost until he finds it?

> (5) When he has found it, he lays it on his shoulders and rejoices.

> (6) And when he comes home, he calls together his friends and neighbors, saying to them, "Rejoice with me, for I have found my sheep that was lost."

Bibliography

Allen, Holly Catterton. *Nurturing Children's Spirituality: Christian Perspectives and Best Practices*. Eugene, OR: Cascade Books, 2008.
Allender, Dan B. *How Children Raise Parents: The Art of Listening to Your Family*. Colorado Springs: Waterbrook Press, 2003.
Bajema, Edith. *A Family Affair: Worshipping God with Our Children*. Grand Rapids: CRC Publications, 1994.
Berryman, Jerome W. *Children and the Theologians: Clearing the Way for Grace*. New York: Morehouse Publishing, 2009.
———. *Godly Play:* New York: Church Publishing Incorporated, 2009.
Cameron, Donald C. *Let the Little Children Come to Me . . . : Children Come to Christian Worship*. St. Joseph, MO: Viaticum Press, 1994.
Carmichael, William, and Nancy Carmichael. *Lord Bless My Child: A Keepsake Prayer Journal to Pray for the Character of God in My Child*. Wheaton, IL: Tyndale House Publishers, 1995.
Cavalletti, Coulter, et al. *The Good Shepherd & The Child: A Joyful Journey*. Oak Park, IL: Catechesis of the Good Shepherd Publications, 1996.
Cavalletti, Sofia. *The Religious Potential of the Child*. New York: Paulist Press, 1979.
———. *The Religious Potential of the Child: 6 to 12 Years Old*. Chicago: Liturgy Training Publications, 2002.
Christie, Ernie. *Coming Home: A Guide to Teaching Christian Meditation to Children*. Singapore: Medio Media, 2008.
Christopher, Doris. *Come to the Table: A Celebration of Family Life*. New York: Warner Books, 1999.
Cloyd, Betty Shannon. *Children and Prayer: A Shared Pilgrimage*. Nashville: Upper Room Books, 1997.
Coles, Robert. *The Moral Intelligence of Children: How to Raise a Moral Child*. New York: Random House, 1997.
———. *The Spiritual Life of Children*. Boston: Houghton Mifflin Company, 1990.
Conde-Frazier, Kang, et al. *A Many Colored Kingdom: Multicultural Dynamics for Spiritual Formation*. Grand Rapids: Baker Academic, 2004.
DeMello, Anthony, S.J. *Sadhana: A Way to God*. New York: Doubleday Publications, 1978.
Eyre, Linda, and Richard Eyre. *Teaching Your Children Joy*. New York: Simon & Schuster, 1994.
Fay, Martha. *Do Children Need Religion?* New York: Pantheon Books, 1993.
Fitzpatrick, Jean Grasso. *Something More: Nurturing Your Child's Spiritual Growth*. New York: Penguin Books, 1992.
Fosarelli, Patricia D. *A.S.A.P: Ages, Stages, and Phases from Infancy to Adolescence*. Liguori, MO: Liguori Publications, 2006.

Bibliography

Fox, Matthew. *Original Blessing: A Primer in Christian Spirituality*. Santa Fe, NM: Bear & Company, 1983.
Garborg, Rolf. *The Family Blessing*. Dallas: Word Publishing, 1990.
Hart, Tobin. *The Secret Spiritual World of Children*. Maui, HI: Inner Ocean Publishing, Inc., 2003.
Hay, David, and Rebecca Nye. *The Spirit of the Child*. London: Jessica Kingsley Publishers, 2006.
Heller, David. *Talking to Your Child About God*. New York: Berkley Publishing Group, 1988.
Hexham, Irving. *Concise Dictionary of Religion*. Downers Grove, IL: Intervarsity Press, 1993.
Hollander, Annette. *How to Help Your Child Have a Spiritual Life: A Parent's Guide to Inner Development*. New York: Bantam Books, 1980.
Komp, Diane M. *A Window to Heaven*. Grand Rapids: Zondervan Publishing House, 1992.
Landers, Peggy. "What Kids Ask (and Know) About God." *St. Paul Pioneer Press* (August 13, 1993).
Lay-Dopyera, Margaret, and John Dopyera. *Becoming a Teacher of Young Children*. New York: Random House, 1977.
L'Engle, Madeleine. *Walking on Water: Reflections on Faith and Art*. Colorado Springs: Waterbrook Press, 1972.
Linn, Fabricant, et al. *Remembering Our Home: Healing Hurts & Receiving Gifts from Conception to Birth*. Mahwah, New Jersey: Paulist Press, 1999.
———. *Simple Ways to Pray for Healing*. Mahwah, New Jersey: Paulist Press, 1998.
———. *Sleeping with Bread: Holding What Gives You Life*. Mahwah, New Jersey: Paulist Press, 1995.
Loder, James E. *The Logic of the Spirit: Human Development in Theological Perspective*. San Francisco: Jossey-Bass, 1998.
Louv, Richard. *Last Child in the Woods: Saving Our Children From Nature-Deficit Disorder*. Chapel Hill, NC: Algonquin Books of Chapel Hill, 2008.
Maresca, Catherine. *Double Close: The Young Child's Knowledge of God*. Loveland, OH: Treehaus Communications, Inc., 2005.
Mason, Mike. *The Mystery of Children: What Our Kids Teach Us About Childlike Faith*. Colorado Springs: Waterbrook Press, 2001.
May, Posterski, et al. *Children Matter: Celebrating Their Place in the Church, Family, and Community*. Grand Rapids: William B. Eerdmans Publishing Company, 2005.
Meehan, Bridget Mary, and Regina Madonna Oliver. *Heart Talks with Mother God*. Collegeville, MN: Liturgical Press, 1995.
Miller-McLemore, Bonnie J. *Let the Children Come: Reimagining Childhood from a Christian Standpoint*. San Francisco: Jossey-Bass, 2003.
Morganthaler, Shirley K. *Exploring Children's Spiritual Formation: Foundational Issues*. River Forest, IL: Pillars Press, 1999.
Nelson, Gertrud Mueller. *To Dance with God: Family Ritual and Celebration*. New York: Paulist Press, 1986.
Newell, J. Philip. *Listening for the Heartbeat of God*. New York: Paulist Press, 1997.
———. *One Foot in Eden: A Celtic View of the Stages of Life*. New York: Paulist Press, 1999.

Bibliography

Nouwen, Henri J. M. *The Living Reminder: Service and Prayer in Memory of Jesus Christ.* New York: Harper Collins Publishers, 2002.

Piper, John. *Leisure, The Basis of Culture.* New York: Pantheon Books, 1963.

Postema, Donald H. *Space for God: The Study and Practice of Prayer and Spirituality.* Grand Rapids: Board of Publications of the Christian Reformed Church, 1983.

Ratcliff, Donald. *Children's Spirituality: Christian Perspectives, Research, and Applications.* Eugene, Oregon: Cascade Books, 2004.

Rechtschaffen, Stephan. *TimeShifting: Creating More Time to Enjoy Your Life.* New York: Doubleday, 1996.

Robichaud, Anne Marie. "Conquering those nighttime anxieties." Online: http://www.canadianparents.com/article/fear-of-the-dark.

Roehlkepartain, King, et al. *The Handbook of Spiritual Development in Childhood and Adolescence.* Thousand Oaks, CA: Sage Publications, 2006.

Smalley, Gary, and John Trent. *The Blessing.* Nashville: Thomas Nelson Publishers, 1986.

Sinetar, Marsha. *Spiritual Intelligence: What We Can Learn from the Early Awakening Child.* Mary Knoll: Orbis Books, 2000.

Smith, Judy Gattis. *Developing a Child's Spiritual Growth Through Sight, Sound, Taste, Touch & Smell.* Prescott, AZ: Educational Ministries, 1996.

———. *Teaching to Wonder: Spiritual Growth Through Imagination and Movement.* Nashville: Abingdon Press, 1990.

Stewart, Sonja M., and Jerome Berryman. *Young Children and Worship.* Louisville, Kentucky: Westminster John Knox Press, 1989.

Stonehouse, Catherine. *Joining Children on the Spiritual Journey: Nurturing a Life of Faith.* Grand Rapids: Baker Books, 1998.

Thompson, Marjorie J. *Family the Forming Center: A Vision of the Role of Family in Spiritual Formation.* Nashville: Upper Room Books, 1996.

Tripp, Tedd, and Margy Tripp. *Instructing a Child's Heart.* Wapwallopen, Pennsylvania: Shepherd Press, 2006.

Turansky, Scott, and Joanne Miller. *Parenting Is Heart Work.* Colorado Springs: Cook Communications Ministries, 2006.

Wangerin, Walter, Jr. *The Orphean Passages: The Drama of Faith.* Grand Rapids: Zondervan, 1996.

Ward, Jennifer. *I Love Dirt: 52 Activities to Help You and Your Kids Discover the Wonders of Nature.* Boston: Trumpeter, 2008.

Webb-Mitchell, Brett. *God Plays Piano, Too: The Spiritual Lives of Disabled Children.* New York: Crossroad Publishing Company, 1993.

Wiederkehr, Macrina. *A Tree Full of Angels: Seeing the Holy in the Ordinary.* San Francisco: HarperCollins, 1988.

Wilkins, Rob. *Taking the Child's Way Home.* Grand Rapids: Zondervan, 1995.

Yust, Johnson, et al. *Nurturing Child and Adolescent Spirituality: Perspectives from the World's Religious Traditions.* Lanham, MD: Rowman and Littlefield Publishers, 2006.

Zimmerman, Martha. *Celebrate the Feasts of the Old Testament in Your Own Home or Church.* Minneapolis: Bethany House Publishers 1981.

www.ingramcontent.com/pod-product-compliance
Lightning Source LLC
Chambersburg PA
CBHW060822190426
43197CB00038B/2183